100 PERFECT PLANTS

A Simple Plan for Your Dream Garden

Simon Akeroyd

National Trust

First published in the United Kingdom in 2017 by

National Trust Books
43 Great Ormond St
London WC1N 3HZ

An imprint of Pavilion Books Group Ltd

ISBN: 9781909881952

A CIP catalogue record for this book is available from the
British Library.

10 9 8 7 6 5 4 3 2 1

Reproduction by Mission, Hong Kong
Printed by 1010 Printing International Ltd, China

This book can be ordered direct from the publisher
at the website: www.pavilionbooks.com, or try your local
bookshop. Also available at National Trust shops or
www.nationaltrustbooks.co.uk.

CONTENTS

INTRODUCTION

How it all started

While relaxing in the kitchen not so long ago, my ten-year-old daughter just happened to ask me what my favourite plant is, in the world, ever, ever! It should be such an easy question for a gardener to answer, but after pausing to think, I realised I didn't have a clue. You see, choosing one favourite plant is almost impossible. As a gardener I work with thousands of different plants of all shapes and sizes, and each one has its own unique character. In fact, in one of the gardens I am responsible for, Agatha Christie's Greenway, there are over 3,000 different types of plants on the estate, so how can I possibly choose just one favourite? It's like asking a mother to choose between her children, or making a child in a sweet factory decide which treat they like the best.

The only way to answer my daughter, eventually, was to list all my favourite plants, which turned out to be a lengthy process. She went to bed a few hours later with a slightly glazed expression on her face and a determination never to ask me another gardening question again!

The bare bones of the list I made on the kitchen table that evening is almost what appears here in this book, except for a number of adjustments made during the writing process. As I began *100 Perfect Plants*, it stirred memories of other plants in other gardens I had encountered. There were some I had fallen in love with but had since forgotten, others I've come to blows with and we'd gone our separate ways for a while, but found each other again. Others still, I was once comfortable with but ultimately discarded, because they've become over-familiar and over-used or I've found a more exciting and showy substitute to inspire me.

Plant perfection personified

So what is a perfect plant? Well, let's face it, as far I'm aware, nothing is perfect. But even after accepting that complete perfection is unachievable, I still had to grapple hard with which plants should make the final cut! After all, appreciation of a plant is very subjective and sometimes it is the very imperfections in something that create the attraction in the first place.

Usually, for something to appeal to us, it needs to entice more than one of our senses. We tend, as gardeners, to concentrate on plants purely for their visual

appearance and beauty, but sometimes our favourite plants appeal to the other senses, too. Many of us have subconsciously chosen a plant because of its scent – a chocolate cosmos, a scented rose or a lemon verbena. In purely sensory terms the fragrance of a flower is usually the most evocative and arousing of all, conjuring up feelings of happiness, nostalgia and a plethora of other emotions and memories.

Ask a cook to choose their favourite plant, and they will almost certainly choose something that tastes sensational, like the honeyed flavour of a Cox's orange pippin apple or a lush Rochester peach picked warm and juicy from the greenhouse. Others might prefer the tactile feel of a plant; the coarseness of *Gunnera manicata* or the soft, velvety feel of the foliage of *Stachys byzantina*. Even sound can play a part in our enjoyment of plants. For some people there may be nothing better than the rustling sounds of bamboos and grasses in the summer breeze.

What makes us call something 'perfect' is often the sum of all parts and how all the elements come together as a whole. At other times it is a single aspect that you become besotted with. Like a difficult actress, one single, fleeting performance for one glorious moment is so spectacular you can forgive the petulant moods and the inevitable sulkiness when she is out of the limelight for the rest of the season.

I have tried to feature both kinds of plants; the instant but short-lived gratification of the truly spectacular performers, as well as those plants that provide interest for much of the garden year, but with no single particular wow factor moment.

Above The spectacular rill garden at Coleton Fishacre is one of the gardens I manage and features many of my favourite plants.

My love is like a rose

Considering there are over 70,000 plants available to buy in garden centres and nurseries across Britain, trying to condense it down to just 100 is very difficult. There are many plants I could have chosen to make the top 100, which I am personally and sentimentally very attached to, yet they did not make the final cut.

As the saying goes, you always remember the first time you fall in love. I first saw her at RHS Wisley Gardens when I was about ten years old. I was bowled over, and felt my heart starting to beat so hard I imagined everybody nearby could hear it. She was called Rose, or should I say *Rosa mundi* and I couldn't take my eyes off her! I was fascinated by the swirly, raspberry ripple colours, and thought it incredible that nature could create something so quirky and colourful. I bought her for £1 (with my mum's financial assistance) and planted her at home. Wherever I've moved to since, I've always taken cuttings and ensured I've got one of them growing in my garden. This deep affection persists, and this is despite that fact that there are far more reliable roses out there, with better disease resistance and flowers for far longer in the season. For this reason, sadly *Rosa mundi* didn't make it into this book, yet it always holds a special place in my heart as my first true love.

The final selection

There were a few practical reasons for my final selection in this book; I wanted to choose a range of plants that offered seasonal interest, I have chosen plants that should be easily available to buy. I have tried to select plants that are hardy and don't require exceptionally mild climates or a greenhouse to grow them in. All the plants featured in this book are fairly reliable and easy to grow although it will be necessary to check their individual requirements and preferences. With regard to trees and shrubs, I've picked plants that won't get too big for your own garden. So, for example, there are no large oak trees or impressive cedars of Lebanon. If you are lucky enough to have a huge, sweeping estate with lakes, bridges and acres of parkland then this may not be the book for you, although I hope you might still find some inspiration for your borders and shrub beds.

Mostly, though, I've chosen plants that make me happy. They're plants that, when I see them in the garden, cheer me up if I've had a bad day. They're plants that make the world a joy to live in. I have been very lucky and privileged to spend my career working as a gardener, being surrounded by beauty every day. I hope the plants in this book give you as much pleasure and joy as they have given to me and thousands of others who come to enjoy them in our gardens at the National Trust. Perhaps nothing really is perfect in the true sense of the word, but I believe that having some of these plants in your garden will help make your life as close to perfect as you can get.

Opposite left Rosa mundi is one of the first plants that fired my passion for gardening. I still grow it in every garden I move to.

Opposite right A perfect plant is hard to define. Ask a chef and they would probably choose something from a fruit or veggie garden.

Opposite below Not all perfect plants take centre stage by producing beautiful flowers. Some are chosen for their foliage, texture or for being a wonderful all-year-round support.

SPRING

THE SEASON AWAKES and you can almost witness the garden moving before your eyes, as foliage, stems and flowers start to unfurl, as if stretching after a deep sleep. Possibly one of the most exciting seasons in the gardening calendar, spring packs a real floral punch with a plethora of plants creating interest from March until May.

There is a sense of anticipation in the air as the garden awakes from its winter slumbers and gardeners feel like they're at the start of another exciting growing season. Bright colours are the main ingredient at this time of year with so many groups of plants creating the wow factor in the garden. The bulbs start to push up through the ground, carpeting lawns and flower beds with colour. Firstly there are the daffodils and crocus, then hyacinths and bluebells and finishing off with the brightly coloured tulips. Another key plant group at this time of year are the spring flowering shrubs, which are predominantly the rhododendrons (including azaleas), magnolias and camellias. However, there is plenty of other interest out there, such as the wonderful tree peonies with their huge, richly coloured flowerheads. Love is in the air too with strings of bleeding hearts appearing in the flower border from *Lamprocapnos spectabilis* (formerly *Dicentra spectablis*) with their impressive display of rose-red, heart-shaped flowers.

Fruit trees are also putting on their magical floral display in the garden, particularly apple, pear and plum blossom. The ornamental apple (*Malus*) and cherry (*Prunus*) trees also create another wow. For impressive climbing displays there are some wonderful clematis at this time of year, such as the evergreen *C. armandii* with its white, scented flowers and the spectacular wisteria with its huge racemes of blue, white or pink flowers.

Previous page The common columbine (*Aquilegia vulgaris*).

Right The garden at A la Ronde, Devon.

1 MAGNOLIA STELLATA, STAR MAGNOLIA

MAGNOLIAS ARE OFTEN CONSIDERED TO BE THE ARISTOCRATS OF THE GARDENING WORLD, BEING ONE OF THE EARLIEST FLOWERING SHRUBS TO BE MENTIONED IN HISTORY. SOME PRODUCE HUGE FLOWERHEADS, OTHERS ARE EVERGREEN WITH LARGE, IMPRESSIVE, GLOSSY FOLIAGE.

Originating from Japan, *Magnolia stellata* is one of the more compact types of magnolia, making it suitable for small gardens or courtyards and balconies. They are also suitable for growing in containers. *M. stellata* is slow growing, only reaching about 2m after about ten years and about 3m wide. It produces scented, white, star-shaped flowers (hence the name *stellata*) in mid spring, although this species can be prone to form a pinkish variation of the pure white. It has quite a twiggy habit, which results in masses of flowers on its bare stems. It can also produce a reddish fruit (inedible) in autumn. Like most magnolias, they prefer slightly acidic soil conditions although *stellata* are more tolerant of

alkaline soil than most. It should be planted in full sun or partial shade, but it does require a sheltered site to ensure its early display of flowers is not destroyed or damaged by strong winds and driving rain. *M. stellata* will also tolerate damp soil, as its original habitat is along the steamy sides and boggy ground of Japan's largest island, Honshu.

Magnolias require very little maintenance. Keep the shrub weed free around its base. Avoid pruning where possible and only do so if it is necessary to tidy up a straggly looking plant, or to remove dead branches. The best time to prune is midsummer when the plant is in full leaf.

ALTERNATIVES

There are a few varieties of the species *stellata* worth trying, including *M. stellata* 'Royal Star' with attractive pale pink buds, opening to masses of elongated white petals. The variety 'Jane Platt' produces rich pink flowers that fade to pale pink, and has a delicate scent. Other types of magnolias to try include the early flowering *M. campbellii*, which produces huge pink flowers in late winter and early spring. However the tree can eventually get quite large so is only suitable for medium or big gardens. *M.* x *loebneri* 'Leonard Messel' is a smaller, rounded tree growing up to 8m high with masses of star-shaped, pale pink flowers. The two most popular evergreen magnolias are *M. grandiflora* and *M. delavayi*, both of which will tolerate dry soil. *M. grandiflora* is suitable for growing against the wall of house and produces heavenly scented, large white flowers that smell of a concoction of vanilla and lemon.

2

PRUNUS 'SHOGETSU', BLUSHING BRIDE

ORNAMENTAL CHERRY TREES PRODUCE SPECTACULAR DISPLAYS OF BLOSSOM RANGING IN COLOUR FROM PALE WHITE TO BRIGHT PINK. THE SIGHT OF THEM IN FLOWER IS SO IMPRESSIVE THAT IN JAPAN, THEY HAVE FESTIVALS TO CELEBRATE THEIR FLOWERING, CALLED HANAMI.

Prunus 'Shogetsu' (commonly Blushing Bride) is one of the most impressive of all the ornamental cherries and the best way to view them is looking up the tree against a clear blue sky. The eventual height of the tree is about 5m (16½ft), making it suitable for small- to medium-sized gardens. It has a typical 'ornamental cherry' tree shape with elegant, wide spreading branches, making it look like there are mini clusters of clouds held aloft above the garden. The result is a tree that is usually broader than it is tall, often as wide as 7m (23ft) across. Its common name is Blushing Bride, because the large, cascading clusters of white double flowers are tinged with an attractive pinkish red colour at first, but when they open fully are a pure white. The foliage provides an additional display in autumn with impressive tinges of red and orange.

Ornamental cherries prefer full sun but will tolerate a moderate amount of dappled shade. However, they require a sheltered position to ensure their blossom isn't damaged by prevailing winds. They require a fertile but well-drained soil and hate having their roots in damp conditions. Keep the tree regularly watered after planting and mulch around the base of the trunk each year in early spring for its first few years, until established. Like the fruiting cherry trees, pruning should only take place when it is in full leaf. Avoid pruning when the tree is dormant during winter as it can succumb to disease.

ALTERNATIVES

P. 'Shirofugen' is an old favourite, in fact about 500 years old. It is a vigorous, wide spreading tree with large, double white fragrant flowers. An added bonus is the copper-coloured leaves, which makes an attractive contrast to the blossom.

'Tai Haku' is known as the Great White Cherry, and is probably the most famous Japanese cherry tree of all. It has large, single, pure white flowers with attractive copper-coloured young foliage. A few of these trees planted in a medium to large garden in full blossom is simply a breathtaking sight. 'Ukon' is worth trying as it has unusual semi-double pale yellow blossom appearing from early to mid-spring with attractive, brownish bronze young foliage.

If you want a cherry tree that will produce delicious fruit then choose 'Stella', which is a self-fertile variety with large, dark red berries in midsummer. It is suitable for growing as free-standing tree or in a fan on a sunny, south-facing wall. For ornamental *Prunus* trees with attractive bark, see page 166.

3

THERE IS NOTHING AS IMPRESSIVE AS AN ORNAMENTAL APPLE TREE IN FULL BLOSSOM. HERALDING THE CRESCENDO OF SPRINGTIME, THEY PROVIDE A DOUBLE WHAMMY IN THE GARDEN, FORMING ATTRACTIVE CRAB APPLES IN AUTUMN IN RUBY RED, BRIGHT YELLOW AND PINK.

Malus 'John Downie' is a very popular choice of ornamental apple tree not just with gardeners, but with gourmet cooks too, as the crab apple jelly made from the fruits of this tree in autumn is considered to be the finest. However, the main reason for growing this tree is the impressive blossom display in spring with pinkish flower buds opening to a spectacular display of white flowers. Large bright orange and red fruits appear in autumn. If they're not harvested for cooking, they can be left for the wildlife to enjoy.

The tree is of a small to medium size with an upright habit, meaning it is suitable for growing in most small gardens. It can also be grown in a pot, but it is important to remember to keep it well watered during the summer. Malus aren't too fussy about where they grow; just avoid compacted soil or boggy ground. Their ideal conditions are well-drained soil in full sun. However, they will tolerate some shade as crab apples don't need to reach the same sugar levels as eating and cooking apples, therefore requiring less sunshine. This is why the

crab apples produced by malus trees should be cooked before eating to make them palatable, due to their lower sugar levels. You could add sugar to them to make crab apple jelly, but they will also make delicious cider if juiced and left to ferment.

Most crab apple trees are self-fertile, meaning that you only need one tree to ensure effective pollination and a bumper crop of fruit in autumn. In addition, because they generally tend to flower for longer than true apple trees, they make effective pollinators for mini orchards and kitchen gardens. Their extended flowering season will also ensure lots of pollinating insects such as bumble and honey bees are attracted to your garden too.

Looking after an ornamental apple tree couldn't be easier. Simply ensure that they have a layer of mulch placed around the base of the tree in early spring. Well-rotted manure or garden compost is the best material to use as they suppress the weeds, retain moisture around the root system and will provide the plant with some additional nutrients.

ALTERNATIVES

There are lots of malus to choose from; in fact this is probably one of the most diverse groups of ornamental fruiting trees due to the range of coloured blossom and fruit produced.

'Golden Hornet' is the other classic traditional ornamental apple tree. It has a broader habit than 'John Downie', and produces large white flowers followed by masses of small, bright yellow crab apples.

M. 'Laura' has spectacular dark red/maroon fruit and attractive pink and white blossom. It has disease resistance to scab and a dwarf habit.

4 CRATAEGUS LAEVEGATA 'PAUL'S SCARLET'

HAWTHORNS ARE ONE OF THE CLASSIC HEDGEROW PLANTS, CHOSEN FOR THEIR DURABILITY, EASE OF GROWING AND ATTRACTIVE SPRING FLOWERS. THEIR DENSE HABIT, ROBUSTNESS AND SHARP THORNS MAKE THEM A POPULAR CHOICE FOR USING AS BOUNDARY MARKERS

Hawthorns are as tough as a pair of old gardening boots. They tolerate most extremes of soil type, urban pollution and some shade. They can also cope with salty coastal conditions and exposed and windy sites. Furthermore, wildlife love this plant, often being used by birds for nesting and feeding on the fruits in autumn, while polluting insects, such as butterflies and bees, are attracted to their flowers in springtime. There are lots of ornamental types, meaning it's possible to combine the plant's practicality with beauty, however, due to its sharp thorns it may be worth avoiding if small children will be playing in the garden.

Crataegus laevegata 'Paul's Scarlet' is one of the most popular ornamental forms of this robust plant. It forms an attractive, small, rounded tree, making it ideal for a small garden. It produces a profusion of double scarlet flowers in spring, followed by attractive red berries later in the year. The fruits can be harvested and made into jams and sauces. As the trunk matures it takes on an attractive, gnarled appearance. Hawthorns hardly need any maintenance; just occasionally prune off any dead or dying branches.

ALTERNATIVES
C. laevegata 'Crimson Cloud' is similar to 'Paul's Scarlet' but produces large, single crimson flowers with white centres and small, bright red fruits. 'Plena' is also similar but produces double white flowers.

5 CERCIS SILIQUASTRUM

THE JUDAS TREE HAS SO MUCH TO OFFER, WITH ATTRACTIVE BUDS, SPECTACULAR FLOWERS, INTRIGUING LOOKING SEED PODS AND WONDERFUL AUTUMN COLOUR. FORMING A SMALL- TO MEDIUM-SIZED TREE, IT WOULD GRACE ANY GARDEN.

This showstopping tree is ideal for a small to medium garden. Commonly known as the Judas tree, it produces masses of pea-like flowers, which begin as startling magenta buds and mature to a stunning, rosy-lilac colour once open. They emerge on bare stems before the foliage appears, giving the tree a real wow factor when in flower. An additional attractive feature of this plant are the purple seed pods that appear later on in the year. The attractive foliage is heart shaped and has soft, buttery-yellow tones in autumn.

Originating from the Mediterranean, *Cercis siliquastrum* prefers a warm sunny site although it can cope with moderate shade. Avoid frost pockets that can damage the early spring flowers. The tree needs to be planted in well-drained soil. Avoid damp conditions.

ALTERNATIVES

Try *C. canadensis* 'Forest Pansy' with its attractive, large purple foliage that feels almost velvety to the touch. It's a wonderful foliage plant, creating the perfect foil or background to shrubs or herbaceous perennials with contrasting colours. A benefit of this shrub over *C. siliquastrum* is that it tolerates shade.

C. siliquastrum 'Alba' is a rarer but equally beautiful form of the Judas tree, which produces white instead of red flowers, and is worth growing if you can track one down.

6

LABURNUM X WATERERI 'VOSSII'

THE SPECTACULAR HANGING CLUSTERS OF GOLDEN-YELLOW FLOWERS ARE A FAMILIAR SIGHT IN SPRING GARDENS UP AND DOWN THE COUNTRY. LABURNUMS ARE VERY VERSATILE AND CAN BE GROWN AS A FREE-STANDING SMALL TREE OR TRAINED LIKE A CLIMBER.

The laburnum is very hardy and a traditional garden favourite. It is one of the highlights of late spring and early summer with its long clusters of fragrant, golden flowers almost dripping from the plant. Most gardeners grow laburnum as a multi-stemmed tree to maximise the amount of flowering branches, which add more interest and structure to a garden design. However, it can be grown as a free-standing tree where it can reach a height of up to 6m (20ft).

The laburnum is very versatile, responding well to pruning. For this reason they are often trained on garden structures, such as pergolas, against walls and fences and in large gardens used to create walkways or tunnels. One of the best examples is the laburnum arch at the National Trust's Bodnant, drawing about 40,000 visitors every year in May to admire it. The arch is 55m (180ft) long, made up of 48 plants, which have been replaced over the years but have provided a continual display of golden flowers in late spring since 1882.

Laburnums aren't too fussy about their soil conditions, and are a good choice for chalky ground where many other specimen trees won't grow. Ideally, they prefer a free-draining but moist soil. They do require full sun though to encourage lots of flowers. Pruning is usually carried out in winter. On free-standing trees this may not be necessary, but if they are being trained up against a wall or arch then some structural pruning will probably be needed.

Understandably, many people have concerns over the fact that laburnums are poisonous, which often overshadows the beauty of the tree, and this has led to many of them being cut down and removed. It is true that all parts of the plant are poisonous, particularly the black seeds contained in the pods, and so it may be best avoided if you have concerns over children who are going to be using the garden.

Voss's laburnum is a spreading deciduous tree and tends to produce fewer of the poisonous seeds than some of the species types. It has longer chains than any other laburnum, growing up to 60cm (2ft) and dark green, clover-like leaves. It is a hybrid of the two most common laburnum species, namely *Laburnum alpinum* (alpine laburnum) and *L. anagyroides* (common laburnum).

ALTERNATIVES

L. alpinum 'Pendulum' creates an attractive, small, weeping or dome-shaped tree, which is ideal for a small garden, making a great focal point.

L. anagyroides 'Aureum' is another attractive laburnum, this one forming golden-yellow leaves in summer as opposed to the usual dark green.

7

CORYLUS AVELLANA 'CONTORTA'

AS WELL AS PROVIDING A BOUNTIFUL SUPPLY OF NUTS IN LATE SUMMER AND EARLY AUTUMN, THIS QUIRKY-LOOKING SHRUB HAS BIZARRE, CONTORTED BRANCHES TO PROVIDE ARCHITECTURAL STRUCTURE IN WINTER AND BEAUTIFUL LONG CATKINS IN SPRING.

If you like the unusual and quirky, then you'll love this curiosity: the corkscrew hazel with its exaggerated, twisted and contorted branches. It is a deciduous shrub, meaning that its dark, tortured and tangled limbs look their best from late autumn through to spring when denuded of leaves. It is much more compact than most other hazel trees, and will tolerate some shade, making it perfect for north-facing gardens or at the back of a shady flower bed. In springtime it produces long tassels of catkins before the green, round foliage appears. The contorted stems and catkins are popular with flower arrangers too.

It makes a superb focus point when grown on its own as a specimen in a small garden with its branches making a wonderful feature when silhouetted against a winter sky. It is also suitable for growing in a pot. However, it also combines well in borders when mixed and contrasted with other small shrubs with spring interest such as *Corylopsis*

pauciflora, rhododendrons or small acers with attractive unfurling young foliage. Plants suitable for underplanting include winter aconites, narcissus, snowdrops and hellebores.

It's ironic that this hazel should have such contorted branches, as the native hazel tree is often grown and harvested for its young, straight sticks, which are used as stakes and plant supports in the garden, particularly for creating wigwams for runner beans to scramble up.

The hazel is naturally a woodland plant, used to growing in the semi-woodland understorey of taller trees, so is tolerant of shade, but will also grow well in full sun. It is slow growing, and although it can eventually reach 5m (16½ft) high, this is only after a good few years and it can be kept in check with regular pruning. In fact it responds well to pruning as it encourages the fresh new growth, which has the best contortions.

ALTERNATIVES

If you're going to grow a hazel tree with the intention of harvesting its nuts, you will need to safeguard against squirrels, which will quickly devour your potential harvest in a blink of an eye.

The traditional native hazel tree is *C. avellana* and there are lots of varieties to try, but my favourite is 'Butler', having large nuts with a strong flavour. Filberts *C. maxima* also make great features in the garden, produce larger nuts than hazels and ripen slightly early on the tree. Both hazels and filberts require pollinators to bear large crops of nuts.

8 CAMELLIA WILLIAMSII 'DONATION'

CAMELLIAS ARE THE QUINTESSENTIAL EARLY SPRING FLOWERING SHRUBS WITH A RANGE OF COLOURFUL, LARGE, SHOWY FLOWERS. THEY ALSO PROVIDE YEAR-ROUND INTEREST AND STRUCTURE WITH THEIR DARK GREEN GLOSSY LEAVES.

Camellia williamsii 'Donation' is an old favourite and one of the most popular camellia varieties, dating back to 1941. This evergreen shrub produces large, semi-double, cup-shaped, orchid-pink flowers. One of the aspects I love about this variety is the profusion of flowers it produces. Shrubs will literally be covered with their blooms in late winter and early spring. It's often described as compact but can get quite large, up to 10m (33ft) high, but they respond well to hard pruning and can be kept compact, ensuring the flowers are closer to the ground and therefore more easily appreciated. A good, manageable height for most camellias in the garden is about 1.5 − 2m (5 − 6½ft) high. The best time to prune a camellia is after flowering, but this is only necessary if the shrub has lost its shape or to restrict its size.

Camellias, like rhododendrons, require an acidic soil to thrive although they may tolerate neutral conditions. Chalky or alkaline soil is definitely to be avoided. If your garden has a high pH then you can still grow camellias in pots where their evergreen, glossy foliage makes for a wonderful feature. If growing in a container they will need to be planted in peat-free ericaceous compost to thrive and should only be watered with rain water (ideally collected in a water butt) in areas with hard mains water. They may also require a liquid feed of sequestered iron if their leaves start to turn yellow.

Remove fading flowerheads as they appear, as this will keep the shrub looking neater, but will also encourage it to produce flowers for longer into springtime.

ALTERNATIVES

There are loads of camellias to try. In fact, at Greenway in Devon where I work, we look after 300 different varieties and this is only scratching the surface of the diversity of this plant group.

Some camellias flower in autumn, such as the species *C. sasanqua*. The variety 'Crimson King' produces fragrant, single red flowers with a yellow centre. *C. sasanqua* 'Autumn Sun' is similar, with fragrant, single pink flowers.

C. japonica 'Bob Hope' is a popular spring flowering shrub with large, semi-double, deep red flowers.

C. 'Cornish Snow' (*cuspidata* × *saluenensis*) is an attractive shrub producing a profusion of small, single white flowers in early to mid-spring.

9 RHODODENDRON 'HYDON DAWN'

RHODODENDRONS COME IN ALL SHAPES AND SIZES, RANGING FROM COMPACT YAKUSHIMANUM VARIETIES, TO LARGER SPECIES TYPES FROM THE HIMALAYAS. WHICHEVER YOU CHOSE, YOU ARE GUARANTEED A PROFUSION OF FLOWERS AND A HUGE SPLASH OF COLOUR.

There are so many rhododendrons to choose from, including both deciduous and evergreen azaleas. Some have the added bonus of being scented, such as *Rhododendron fragrantissimum* and the azalea *R. luteum*, while others have attractive indumentum (felt-like appearance) on the underside or topside of their leaves, often in copper, white or even gold.

R. 'Hydon Dawn' is suitable for small gardens as it forms a compact shape, reaching about 1.5m (5ft) high and across. It is one of the Yak-type hybrids (yakushimanum), which were bred for their small size and to produce masses of flowers. In fact, in springtime, it is practically impossible to find a place on its branches that isn't covered. An evergreen shrub that produces amazing frilly, light pink flowers, it has the additional bonus of a blueish cream indumentum on its beautiful glossy leaves.

Like all rhododendrons it prefers acidic, slightly moist, but free-draining soil. It prefers dappled shade, but it will cope with full sun if the soil is damp enough.

Rhododendrons are in need of a publicity makeover. The invasive *R. ponticum* has caused problems in the countryside, smothering out any surrounding plants and opportunities for wildlife. Yet, most rhododendrons are fine to grow in a garden, and do not have the same spreading tendencies, making them wonderful flowering specimens, requiring very little maintenance. Many people associate rhododendrons with out-of-date, 1970s gardening, but thankfully woodland gardens are now very much back in fashion, and these are the perfect plants to replicate this style, requiring just one or two plants in a small- to medium-sized garden.

Deadheading as flowers fade makes the plant look tidier, extends the flowering season and encourages the formation of flower buds for the following year too. It isn't necessary to prune 'Hydon Dawn', just occasionally remove a branch or give it a trim with secateurs if it loses its shape. During its initial couple of years after planting it will benefit from a mulch of rotted pine needles or peat-free ericaceous compost at the base of its trunk.

ALTERNATIVES

There are simply loads to try, in all shapes and sizes. 'Hydon Hunter' is similar to 'Hydon Dawn', but has bright pink flowers with spotty orange markings on the inside of the flower. If you want to try something a bit bigger than 'Hydon Dawn', try *R.* 'Purple Sensation', which is a medium to large evergreen shrub growing up to 3m (10ft), with rich purple flowers in spring and dark markings on the throats of the flowers.

If you live in a mild climate the medium-sized shrub *R. fragrantissimum* is a must. It has a gorgeous fragrance in spring produced from attractive whitish pink flowers with a yellow throat.

10

KERRIA JAPONICA 'PLENIFLORA'

KERRIA IS ONE OF THE UBIQUITOUS SPRINGTIME SHRUBS WITH ARCHING STEMS LOADED WITH BRIGHTLY COLOURED YELLOW FLOWERS. IT ORIGINATES FROM CHINA, JAPAN AND KOREA, AND IS NAMED AFTER THE PLANT COLLECTOR WILLIAM KERR.

Yellow is a popular colour in springtime, with daffodils smothering the ground and slightly higher up in the line of sight forsythia and the kerria shrub all flowering profusely and taking centre stage. Kerria is a deciduous shrub that is commonly seen in many front gardens in towns and cities, and often appears in cottage gardens, with its slightly sprawling habit and its high-impact colour. Sometimes known as the Japanese rose, kerria is named after the plant collector William Kerr, who introduced *Kerria* 'Pleniflora' in the early nineteenth century after being sent off to China by the East India Company to seek out new plants.

Kerria is perfect for illuminating a dark and shady corner of any garden with its brightly coloured flowers. One of its benefits is its ability to grow almost anywhere. So if you have poor, impoverished soil in your garden, this could be an ideal choice of plant. In fact, one of the downsides is that it can almost be difficult to get it to stop growing and it sends out lots of suckers, which will need to be removed to keep the plant in check. It is a tough plant, very hardy and will tolerate exposed sites.

'Pleniflora' is an attractive variety of kerria as it produces double golden-yellow flowers on its graceful, arching stems. The leaves are bright green, oval and toothed. It's fast growing so if you want a shrub that will quickly cover an unsightly wall or fence then this shrub is ideal. Even though the plant is deciduous the dense thicket of canes produced during summer will provide some screening in winter. Thankfully, despite the plant's vigour, it doesn't get too big, reaching an overall height of 3 – 4m (10 – 13ft) if left unpruned.

Maintenance is very easy with kerria. Simply remove some of the older stems after flowering at ground level. Also, remove any other suckers that are starting to creep away from where the shrub is intended to be grown.

Kerria grows best in shade as the flowers can become slightly bleached in direct sunlight. Although it will survive in most soils, it prefers a moist but well-drained soil.

ALTERNATIVES

K. japonica 'Golden Guinea' and 'Simplex' are other popular varieties that are covered with single, bright yellow flowers in spring. 'Picta' is a more unusual type of kerria, producing silver variegated foliage and is slightly less vigorous.

Try the deciduous shrub forsythia for a similar splash of yellow in the garden, but slightly less vigorous than kerria.

11 AMELANCHIER LAMARCKII

AMELANCHIER LAMARCKII IS A WONDERFUL SHRUB OFFERING SEVERAL PERIODS OF INTEREST IN THE YEAR, RANGING FROM ITS MULTI-STEMMED STRUCTURE IN WINTER, VIBRANT COLOURED FOLIAGE IN AUTUMN, AND ATTRACTIVE BERRIES.

If you only have room in your garden for one shrub then this should probably be it as it offers so many seasons of interest. Snowy mespilus, as it is commonly known, originates from eastern North America, and due to its graceful habit it is an ideal choice for a central feature in a garden, or to slot into an awkward corner or space.

It's an incredibly versatile tree and responds well to pruning, meaning it can be pruned to suit style and taste in an overall garden design. Most people grow it as a multi-stemmed tree by pruning it back hard when young to encourage lots of growth. However, it can be left to form an attractive small tree with a single trunk and wide spreading crown. Because of this versatility it is suitable for both informal, cottage garden-type gardens and formal settings where it can be used to punctuate plant displays with its architectural structure. It can even be used to create tree-lined avenues alongside urban paths and roads.

Unusually there are two seasons of foliage interest, as not only does it have attractive autumn colours, but the juvenile spring growth also has an unusual reddish or bronze colour. However, its main feature is its mass of white, star-shaped flowers. It is so impressive that a cluster or avenue of the trees in full blossom will give most malus a run for their money.

Snowy mespilus is relatively trouble free but it doesn't like chalky or lime soil and can struggle in very dry conditions. The ideal soil is moist and free draining. It prefers full sun but will tolerate partial shade.

An additional benefit of *Amelanchier lamarckii* is that wildlife love feeding on the dark, reddish purple berries, which is ideal if you enjoy watching birds. The berries usually appear from mid- to late summer, have a sweet taste and are worth trying if you can get to them before the birds.

ALTERNATIVES

A. x *grandiflora* 'Robin Hill' is an upright small tree, which produces pink flowers that fade to white and are followed by dark purple berries. It has a showy autumn foliage display with fiery colours of orange and red. Its early spring foliage is an attractive bronze colour.

A. 'La Paloma' is an attractive large shrub with deep bronze foliage and lots of sprays of white flowers in spring. The foliage provides interest and bright colours in autumn.

One of my favourites is *A.* x *grandiflora* 'Ballerina', which forms a large shrub with bronze young foliage that turns orange and purple in autumn. In spring it produces racemes of white flowers and, later, small, reddish purple fruit.

12 EXOCHORDA X MACRANTHA 'THE BRIDE'

KNOWN AS 'THE BRIDE' BECAUSE IN SPRING THIS EXQUISITELY
FRAGRANT SHRUB IS SIMPLY COVERED FROM HEAD TO FOOT WITH
CLUSTERS OF PURE WHITE, FRILLY FLOWERS. ITS FLOWING AND CURVY
SHAPE MAKES IT REMINISCENT OF A TRADITIONAL BRIDAL DRESS.

Often known as the pearlbush as its opening buds resemble pearls, this is a deciduous spreading shrub with a graceful arching habit. It is native of China and central Asia and is fully hardy. It only reaches 2m (6½ft) tall but can get up to 3 – 4m (10 – 13ft) wide. It works really well when planted at the back of a flower border, where its pure white flowers and oval, fresh green leaves make an excellent foil for brighter coloured plants in the foreground. Planting it next to a purple-coloured foliage plant, such as *Cotinus coggygria* or *Cercis canadensis* 'Forest Pansy' makes a striking contrast.

If possible plant it near an outside dining area, patio or bench to enjoy its early summer fragrance, which will perfume the air.

'The Bride' prefers full sun in moist but well-drained soil. Avoid chalky and limy soil and shallow ground.

Add plenty of organic matter prior to planting. It requires minimal pruning unless it's necessary to contain its spreading habit. Some of the older wood can be removed immediately after flowering to encourage replacement arching young stems. Flowers appear in late spring and early summer.

ALTERNATIVES

'The Bride' is by far the most popular exochorda to be found in garden centres, but there are a few others worth trying. For example, *E. giraldii* var. *wilsonii* is native to central China and slightly rarer and has large paper-white flowers in late spring/early summer. Even rarer (but it shouldn't be) is *E. serratifolia* 'Snow White', which is native to Korea and Manchuria, and produces pure-white flowers freely in early spring.

(Note: 'The Bride' is often confused with *Spiraea arguta* purely because its common name is the bridal wreath shrub. However, this spirea is also an attractive shrub, forming beautiful late spring/early summer white flowers on slender, arching branches.)

13 VIOLA TRICOLOR

DIMINUTIVE AND EASILY OVERLOOKED, OUR NATIVE WILD PANSY IS NEVERTHELESS A CHARMING LITTLE PLANT, WITH THE ADDED ATTRACTION OF SOME OF THE MOST WONDERFUL COMMON NAMES IN THE HORTICULTURAL LANGUAGE.

Only 15cm (6in) high, *Viola tricolor* packs a lot of colour into a small space, with a neat little face painted purple, white and yellow. It will first flower in spring but, through rapid self-seeding, will continue to produce new plants throughout the season that in turn will flower and set seed themselves.

It is an unfussy plant, enjoying sunshine and indifferent to a lack of water. It will just flower and seed all the quicker. Its self-seeding is rarely a real problem as it is such a small plant it will never outcompete the bigger, more fussy and exacting plants you might have around.

The most popular common name for this plant is 'heartsease' but it has also been known as 'tickle-my-fancy', 'Jack-jump-up-and-kiss-me' and 'love-in-idleness'. Whether its association with matters of the heart is just a classical myth or a result of being gathered for free from the hedgerows by many a

poor shepherd wooing an unsuspecting maiden we can never be sure. Shakespeare certainly thought it made a powerful love potion.

ALTERNATIVES
Modern breeding has transformed the wild heartsease into a number of pansy series with a wide range of colours and bigger blooms. The 'Sorbet' series, for example, are single colour pansies with no eye in the centre that flower in late winter and spring. *V.* x *wittrockiana* 'Sorbet Black Delight' makes a perfect foil to early yellow narcissus.

For a woodland and natural garden *V. odorata*, the sweet violet, is essential, colonising dappled shade by seed and spreading rhizomes.

OFTEN REFERRED TO AS GRANNY'S BONNETS DUE TO THE SHAPE OF THEIR FLOWERHEADS, AQUILEGIAS ARE THE ARCHETYPAL COTTAGE GARDEN PLANT. THEY'RE SIMPLE TO GROW, COME IN A RANGE OF DIFFERENT COLOURS AND CAN BE EASILY PROPAGATED FROM SEED.

The bell-shaped flowers of aquilegia come in a wide range of colours and some varieties produce striking looking spurs at the back of the flowerheads. They are fully hardy and thrive in full sun or light shade. Their attractive, deeply-cut, decorative foliage looks great in summer, even when the flowers have faded.

Aquilegia 'Nora Barlow' is one of the oldest forms of aquilegia and is named after Charles Darwin's grand-daughter. However, records of it date back to the seventeenth century, when it was known as the rose columbine. This one has dark green divided leaves with thickly clustered, spurless double flowers about 2.5cm (1in) across, composed of narrow petals of soft pink and white with green tips. It requires a well-drained but moist soil in full sun or partial shade. Plant in groups of three, five or seven for the most dramatic effect in the border.

Aquilegias are very promiscuous and will quickly spread throughout your garden. If you want to stop them self-seeding it is best to cut down the stems as soon as they have finished flowering. However, one tip to increase your planting stock is to allow them to turn to seed and then shake them over gaps in your planting schemes in late summer or early autumn. Their willingness to germinate will ensure that your beds are fully stocked the following year. They will cross-pollinate with other varieties and species, so if there are any other types in your garden, or those of your neighbours, you may find yourself with a brand-new, exclusive variety.

Aquilegias are clump-forming perennials and grow up to about 80cm (2½ft) in height. They are short lived perennials but easy to maintain, simply cutting back the stem after flowering. They look fantastic when their flowers appear to be hovering over spring flowering bulbs, such as grape hyacinths and daffodils. I like to see their attractive leaves contrasted next to bright yellow tulips or the feathery foliage of bronze fennel.

ALTERNATIVES

If you want the traditional, cottage garden columbine, then grow the plain species *A. vulgaris*, which is blue or white and has short spurs.

   A. vulgaris 'William Guinness' has impressive velvety-red outer petals and spurs, with pale pink and white inner cup-shaped flowers.

   A. vulgaris 'Nivea' is a white-flowered aquilegia with short spurs and ideal for cottage gardens or light woodland. It's sometimes also called 'Munstead's White'.

   For something a bit brighter try 'Crimson Star' that has bright red flowers with a yellow centre.

15 EUPHORBIA EPITHYMOIDES

SPRINGTIME IS OFTEN A QUIET TIME IN THE HERBACEOUS BORDER, BUT THE PERENNIAL EUPHORBIA EPITHYMOIDES PROVIDES BOLD BLOCKS OF COLOUR, WITH ITS STRIKING, GREENISH YELLOW FOLIAGE AND ACIDIC YELLOW FLOWER BRACTS.

There are lots of euphorbias to choose from, but none so bold and bolshie as this early performer in the herbaceous border. It is an evergreen perennial, which forms attractive, rounded clumps of light green foliage. In spring the foliage is covered with effervescent yellow flowers that almost look acidic in colour. It is a really hardy reliable plant for the front of the herbaceous border, and ideal for creating interest at a time of year when little else is happening on the herbaceous perennial front. However, it can start to look a little scruffy later on in the year, so placing it towards the back of the border if nothing else is screening it in early to mid-spring is not a bad option. As it only grows to about 45cm (1½ft) high, it will then be hidden and tucked away when the summer herbaceous border flowers start to grow.

Euphorbia epithymoides originates in open, dry woodlands in Turkey and south-east Europe and can also be seen on mountainous hillsides. For this reason, it prefers a well-drained, light soil and requires full sun, although will tolerate light dappled shade if the soil is moister and enriched with humus. After flowering it is worth trimming back the plant to tidy it up and, depending on the summer climate, it may reward you with another flush of growth. Do be careful not to get the sap on your skin as it is an irritant. To create more plants it can be lifted out of the ground in early autumn and divided into sections before being replanted.

The bright yellow and green foliage of this plant contrasts well with some of the spring blue flowers, such as pulmonarias, bluebells, scillas and even forget-me-nots. Yellow bulbs, such as daffodils, also make great complementary planting. One of my favourite spring plant combinations is with *Paeonia* 'Molly the Witch' whose large, lemon-coloured flowers look great against the bright yellow of the euphorbia.

ALTERNATIVES

There are lots of *E. epithymoides* varieties to choose from if you can't find the original. For something a bit different try 'Candy', as it has attractive, purple-flushed spring foliage; 'Midas' and 'Sonnengold' have almost golden-coloured flower bracts that look amazing during spring. 'Bonfire' has amazing foliage, which turns green and burgundy in summer, then deepens to red by autumn. If you prefer variegated forms there is 'Lacey', which has cream edges to its foliage.

    E. amygdaloides 'Craigieburn', is known as the wood spurge, and as its name suggests is suitable for growing in the shade. The stems are an amazing burgundy colour and the young leaves at the top of the whorly foliage are a deep red that fade to dark green. In spring bright green flower clusters appear, creating a stunning contrast to the dark reds and greens of the foliage below.

COMMONLY KNOWN AS PERIWINKLE, THESE PLANTS MAKE PERFECT GROUND COVER FOR THOSE TRICKY AREAS IN THE GARDEN WHERE LITTLE ELSE GROWS. THEIR SPREADING HABIT MAKES A BEAUTIFUL CARPET OF FOLIAGE AND FLOWERS, AND HELPS TO SUPPRESS WEEDS.

The common periwinkle probably wouldn't be on the top 100 list for most gardeners, but there are a number of reasons why I rate this plant. They are fairly tolerant of pollution, making them ideal for sprawling and rambling in town gardens. They aren't too fussy about soil conditions and they need very little looking after. This plant is a real grafter and just two or three will quickly cover a bare soil. So it's the perfect plant for those people on a tight budget or a short on time.

Although they have a spreading habit, they aren't too hard to control and are much less vigorous than the *major* species of *Vinca*. They are very hardy and will often flower all year round, including in the depths of winter. Ideal for many new-build properties with a load of building rubble buried just below the surface of the soil, it requires very little rooting depth. And surely this ground cover plant, with its attractive foliage and colourful violet-blue flowers, is more interesting than a lawn. It doesn't need cutting once a week during summer either, making it very low maintenance.

It grows in light and dappled shade, although it does prefer a sunny location and will produce more flowers if provided with plenty of light. They are also fairly drought-tolerant. Another reason for loving this plant is its versatility, as it will grow up structures and on walls.

But the main reason why *Vinca minor* makes this book is because at the National Trust's Greenway in Devon, where I look after over 3,000 plants, I get asked by visitors about *V. minor* 'Dartington Star' more than anything else. Visitors love it with its dark blue, almost purple flower, which appears to hover over the dark green foliage. The flower has five pronounced, individual, elongated petals that look so much classier than the standard vinca with its fatter petals. And it flowers for ages, almost all year round, although most of the flowers appear during spring. Even without the pointed, star-shaped flowers, the attractive foliage still provides interest.

Maintenance of *V.* 'Dartington Star' is very easy. They can just be left to their own devices, but I would recommend a light chop with a pair of edging shears (or a hedge trimmer if you prefer) a couple of times a year to keep the plant close to the ground and encourage a new flush of foliage and flowers.

ALTERNATIVES

The plain *V. minor* has lots of merits and is a great ground cover plant with glossy dark leaves and violet-blue flowers for most of the year. *V. major* 'Variegata' is sometimes also sold as 'Elegantissima' and is a sub-shrub that has oval, dark green leaves with creamy white margins and dark violet flowers. It is a great ground cover plant but can be invasive if left to its own devices. *V. minor* 'Atropurpurea' is an attractive, lesser periwinkle type with beautiful plum-purple flowers and dark green leaves. *V. difformis* 'Jenny Pym' is another attractive periwinkle, having light pink and white flowers. It is not as tough as the *minor* and *major* species.

17   LAMPROCAPNOS SPECTABILIS

A WONDERFUL MID- TO LATE SPRINGTIME CLASSIC, THIS HERBACEOUS PERENNIAL HAS ROSY-RED, HEART-SHAPED FLOWERS LADEN ON LONG, ARCHING STEMS. THE BLEEDING HEART PLANT WILL MAKE YOUR HEART SING WITH JOY WHEN IT COMES INTO FLOWER IN YOUR GARDEN.

It's amazing that such a tragically named plant, 'bleeding heart', can make so many people happy when they see it growing in the garden. It is one of the most commonly commented-on plants at the National Trust's Coleton Fishacre, one of the gardens I manage, and I can understand why. The flowers literally look like plump little hearts strung out along a stem, but beneath the 'flower' hangs a white, drip-shaped extension, hence the name bleeding heart. The other name, which I much prefer as it's much cheerier, is 'lady-in-the-bath' and if you turn the flower upside down you can see why it is so named.

Lamprocapnos spectabilis should ideally be planted in dappled shade in moist, well-drained, fertile soil. Not many herbaceous perennials are out in spring so it's always wonderful to see this one appear, heralding the beginning of a new season in the herbaceous border. It grows to about 1.2m (4ft) high and is suitable for growing in the middle or back of the herbaceous border. It looks equally good in informal settings, such as at the edge of a woodland garden or in a cottage garden among spring bulbs, shrubs and early flowering rambling roses, such as the banksia rose. They are surprisingly easy to grow and perfect for lightening up a dark or shady corner in the garden.

Mulch around the plants in late winter to help retain moisture at the base of the plant. Cut back the foliage when it starts to die back from mid- to late summer, although in hot, dry summers it often dies back early, which is worth considering when planning a planting scheme, ensuring that other strong plants are nearby to hide the gap left by the bleeding heart.

ALTERNATIVES
The other bleeding heart commonly found in garden centres is *L. spectabilis* 'Alba', which produces pure white, heart-shaped flowers. My favourite is 'Bacchanal', which has dark crimson 'bleeding hearts'.

18 PULMONARIA 'BLUE ENSIGN'

QUIRKY LOOKING, SPOTTED LEAVES AND MASSES OF BLUE FLOWERS ARE THE HIGHLIGHT OF THIS STRONG GROWING HERBACEOUS PERENNIAL. THEIR GREEN, SILVERY OR GREY FOLIAGE LOOKS GREAT WHEN CONTRASTED AGAINST OTHER FOLIAGE WITH BRIGHTER TONES.

Commonly known as lungwort because in early herbal medicinal history it was believed that the spotted leaves looked similar to diseased lungs and so would be used to treat pulmonary disorders, I cannot recommend this to treat lung problems, however I do suggest growing it in your garden, as it is a beautiful, tough plant and has the enduring ability to produce masses of flowers without even shuddering when there is a harsh spring frost. They make great ground cover plants with their thick, coarse leaves covering up any gaps in flower beds to suppress potential weeds.

Pulmonaria require a cool, shady place so are perfect for tricky corners in small town or courtyard gardens where beds are often shaded by nearby buildings. They're also ideally suited to woodland gardens, or underplanting shrubs, and look perfect in an informal cottage garden. Bees love this plant as an early source of nectar and so are also suitable for planting in wildlife gardens.

Pulmonaria 'Blue Ensign' is a particularly good variety, producing masses of dark, violet-blue flowers throughout spring, and has narrow, dark leaves.

They are fast growing plants and will benefit from being lifted and divided every few years to keep them looking fresh. Trim back the plant each year after flowering to encourage a new flush of growth.

ALTERNATIVES
P. rubra 'Redstart' has bright green, hairy leaves and produces masses of tubular, coral-red flowers in early spring. Sometimes it can flower as early as Christmas.

P. 'Lewis Palmer' produces clusters of pink, funnel-shaped flowers when they open and eventually turn to vibrant blue in mid-spring. The foliage is dark green with white spots.

P. officinalis 'Sissinghurst White' forms pure white spring flowers and white spotted foliage on its dark green leaves.

19

CLEMATIS ARMANDII

THERE ARE CLEMATIS THAT FLOWER IN EVERY SEASON BUT ONE OF THE MOST POPULAR IS THE EVERGREEN AND FRAGRANT CLEMATIS ARMANDII WITH ITS LEATHERY LEAVES AND CREAMY WHITE, STAR-SHAPED FLOWERS.

This clematis was introduced to Britain in 1900 by the wild adventurer and plant hunter Ernest Wilson from China (often called Chinese Wilson). He risked life and limb to introduce many plants to Britain. I feel most guilty about this when relaxing at home at my writing desk with a window open, enjoying the evening spring breeze gently wafting in the almond-like scent from the *armandii* flowering on my outside wall.

This evergreen climber has attractive, long, deep green leaves making it an attractive feature all year round, but really comes into its own in spring when it produces masses of flowers that have an intoxicating but subtle scent. Although it is a climbing plant it does need a support system of wires or trellis. It is very slightly tender so it is best to train it up the south side of a building or wall where it can maximise the sun's rays. Avoid exposed sites and frost pockets.

Clematis armandii should be planted with the top of their crown level with the soil. They like warm heads and cold feet, so try to provide some shade for the base of the plant, which will encourage the plant to grow upwards towards warmer climes. Add plenty of organic matter prior to planting to give it enough clout to climb high and sustain itself. The soil should be moist but free draining. The best time for planting is while the soil is still warm in late summer or early autumn. It may need occasional

watering during the first year to get it established, especially in spring prior to flowering.

Maintenance is simple, just remove any damaged or dead growth once it has finished flowering. It may need retraining and tying onto the wall if it has got too overgrown. Avoid cutting into the old wood.

ALTERNATIVES

C. armandii 'Appleblossom' is one of the most popular *armandii* types, which produces masses of pink-tinged white sprays of flowers in spring and a vanilla scent. The opening buds are also an interesting feature with a more intense pink colour.

20 Wisteria sinensis

PROBABLY THE NATION'S FAVOURITE CLIMBERS, WISTERIA PRODUCE AN ABUNDANCE OF LONG RACEMES OF DEEP BLUE FLOWERS IN SPRING WITH AN INTOXICATING SCENT THAT CONJURES UP IMAGES OF INTREPID EXPLORERS DISCOVERING THIS PLANT IN EXOTIC LANDS.

There is nothing more evocative or romantic than sitting under an arbour with these sweetly perfumed clusters of flowers hanging down, gently swaying in the breeze. There is something almost dreamy, a sublime richness, and a luxuriant atmosphere whenever I encounter this plant. Perhaps it is because of its vivid colour, its sweet scent or perhaps simply nostalgia, evoking a sense of traditional Victorian gardening, combined with the excitement of distant lands. Or maybe, quite simply, it is the intrinsic beauty of wisteria.

Wisteria has a reputation for being tricky to grow because it has to be pruned annually. This is partly true, in fact it should ideally be pruned twice a year, but once the simple technique has been mastered, it will continue to perform and flower its heart out for years to come. The first prune is carried out just after flowering when the new growth is cut back to about 10cm (4in). This is simply to tidy up the plant and allow sunlight into the canopy to encourage the development of flower buds, which will produce more flowers the following spring. Later in winter the new growth is cut back harder to a couple of buds. This is simply to keep the plant tidier and maintain its shape.

Wisteria sinensis is the Chinese form of this plant. It needs a trellis or system of wires to train the plant onto. This species grows or climbs by sending out shoots in an anti-clockwise direction, yet the Japanese wisteria (*W. floribunda*) grows in a clockwise direction. It produces lilac-blue, pea-like flowers held together on long pendant clusters. Flowers appear before the leaves, as opposed to the Japanese species, in which flowers and leaves appear simultaneously. It prefers full sun but will tolerate some shade, so does best on a south-west or south-facing wall. Add plenty of organic matter into the soil prior to planting. It should be planted at the same level it was in the pot. Most wisteria are grafted onto rootstocks so ensure that the union (the bulge on the stem a few centimetres above the rootball) is above the ground.

ALTERNATIVES

The Japanese wisteria (*W. floribunda*) is similar to the Chinese version but produces longer racemes of flowers (up to 45cm/18in long as opposed to 30cm/12in) but they appear at the same time as the foliage. The variety 'Royal Purple' has scented violet flowers that can reach almost 50cm (20in) long in late spring/early summer. 'Alba' produces long racemes of white flowers and 'Rosea' pink ones.

ERYTHRONIUM
'PAGODA'

THE DOG'S TOOTH VIOLET IS A BULBOUS PERENNIAL GROWING UP TO ABOUT 40CM TALL WITH STRIKING STAR-SHAPED PETALS. IT IS EASY TO GROW AND PROBABLY ONE OF THE MOST REWARDING AND GRACEFUL OF ALL THE SPRINGTIME BULBS.

Erythronium 'Pagoda' is a stunning hybrid derived from one of the North American erythroniums. They require moist but free-draining soil and dappled shade to replicate their native, open woodland habitat. Therefore in the garden they are ideal for underplanting shrubs and small trees or placing in a woodland setting. They only reach about 40cm (16in) high so bulbs should be planted near the edges of woodland paths or at the front of a mixed shrub border to ensure they are seen at their best. They produce sulphur yellow, star-shaped flowers with reflexed heads suspended on elegantly arching stems. Their wide, mottled, glossy leaves are another attractive feature of this bulbous perennial.

It is a vigorous plant and quickly reproduces in the ground, bulking up into large clumps by producing young bulb offsets freely, and occasionally underground runners. Erythroniums prefer not to be disturbed once planted. However, if clumps get too large they can be dug up and divided in late summer and early autumn, ensuring the bulbs are planted back immediately to prevent them drying out.

Apparently the name dog's tooth violet comes from the shape of the corm. The best time to plant them is in autumn.

ALTERNATIVES

E. dens-canis is the most popular erythronium and it has mottled leaves with rose-coloured flowers. *E. californicum* 'White Beauty' is one of the most beautiful varieties (closely related to 'Pagoda'). It has pure white flowers with a red centre.

22 Hyacinthoides non-scripta

THE ENGLISH BLUEBELL IS THE QUINTESSENTIAL WOODLAND PLANT WITH ITS DAINTY, NODDING FLOWERHEAD AND DELICATE FRAGRANCE. OFTEN BEST SEEN EN MASSE WHEN NATURALISED IN WOODLAND, BUT THEY LOOK EQUALLY GREAT IN SHADY AREAS IN THE GARDEN.

Masses of blue, nodding flowers far into the distance is a wonderful sight to behold in ancient woodlands during mid- to late spring, but a similar effect can be created on a much smaller scale in the garden. *Hyacinthoides non-scripta* will fill the garden with a gorgeous fragrance and are a source of nectar for bees, moths and butterflies. Being woodland plants they prefer dappled shade and moist but free-draining soil. Their ideal location is beneath deciduous trees where the falling leaf litter in autumn and winter will replicate the forest floor where they naturally thrive. In smaller gardens they can be grown under shrubs and they do tolerate full sun if the soil is moist and fertile enough.

Bulbs should be planted in autumn at least to a depth of between 10 and 15cm (4 and 6in), and about the same apart from each other. To get the 'natural' look in the garden the bulbs should be scattered over the area and planted where they fall. Dig in organic matter such as leaf mould prior to planting.

Bluebells can also be moved during spring when 'in the green', which basically means while still in leaf.

Dig up clumps and plant them at the same depth as they were in the soil before, which will probably be between 10 and 15cm (4 and 6in).

Let the foliage die back naturally after planting. Resist the temptation to cut them back after flowering as they need their foliage to photosynthesise and capture enough energy to send out flowers the following year. Don't despair if bulbs moved while 'in the green' don't flower the following year but instead only send up foliage. This is because the plant is focusing on re-establishing itself in the soil and it may take a couple of years before recovering from the transportation and being willing to flower.

The planting of Spanish bluebells in the garden is a controversial subject in the gardening world. They have larger flowers, which form on a sturdier stem, but have less of a fragrance than English bluebells. The problem is that they are naturalising in the woodlands and either swamping out the native plants, or hybridising with them.

ALTERNATIVES

Grape hyacinths (*Muscari arneniacum*) produce clusters of tiny blue flowers and make a wonderful contrast to yellow spring flowering bulbs, such as yellow hyacinths, daffodils, *Erythronium* 'Pagoda' and winter aconites. They can become a bit invasive and may need management to ensure they don't overrun the garden.

Scilla mischtschenkoana 'Tubergeniana' is a dwarf perennial with strap-like leaves and attractive silvery-blue flowers with dark stripes. Preferring full sun, they are suitable for the front of flower borders or naturalising in grass. *S. bifolia* is another alternative with star-shaped, dark blue or purple flowers. These will tolerate dappled shade and are ideal for naturalising under trees and shrubs.

23 FRITILLARIA MELEAGRIS

THRIVING IN DAMP OPEN GROUND AND MEADOWS, SNAKE'S HEAD FRITILLARY ARE FASCINATING, WITH THEIR CHEQUERED, NODDING HEADS LOOKING LIKE SNAKES' HEADS REARING OUT OF THE GROUND IN LATE SPRING.

These attention-grabbing, fascinating spring bulbs make an impressive sight when their nodding, bell-shaped flowers appear in late spring. The flowers appear about 30cm (12in) above the ground and have a quirky and distinctive chequered pattern, with purple being the predominant colour, but there are lots of permutations of pink and mauve markings and stripes making each flower distinct. There are also those that are mainly white, which are equally delightful. They look at their best when naturalised in grass, but they do require damp conditions to perform well.

If your garden is on heavy clay soil or simply on damp, boggy ground then these native wild flowers could be your solution to providing a splash of colour in the borders or in the lawn. Most other spring bulbs, such as tulips, crocus and grape hyacinths, prefer a more free-draining soil.

Bulbs should be planted in autumn. If planting in grass, scatter them over the surface first to get a naturalised feel, and plant them where they land. They should be planted at least two times the depth of the bulb and at least 20cm (8in) apart from each other. Do bear in mind though that if you plant them in your lawn, you won't be able to mow the grass until their foliage has died down, which might not be ideal if you only have one small lawn. However, they can be naturalised in a small, damp corner or even on the edge of the lawn near a hedge, assuming the soil is damp enough. The bulbs are fully hardy, fairly trouble free and will even seed freely if the conditions are right.

If you don't have a lawn then you can try growing *Fritillaria meleagris* in containers, but they will need watering regularly to ensure the soil is damp enough for them to thrive.

ALTERNATIVES

I love *F.graeca* and I'm surprised it isn't in more people's gardens. It originates from Greece yet is fully hardy and produces nodding, bell-shaped flowers that are similar to the snake's heads, but their colour is brownish purple with very distinctive green stripes. It requires full sun and good drainage but looks fantastic when grown in a rockery, gravel bed, dry garden or even at the front of raised beds.

At the opposite scale in terms of size to the dainty snake's head fritillaries are the more imposing and larger crown fritillaries, *F. imperialis*. These bulbous perennials appear in late spring with their tall, dark purple stems over 1m (3ft) high, carrying aloft their large, colourful, bell-shaped flowers, above which sit clusters of leaves that look like a spiky hair-do (the crown).

24 NARCISSUS POETICUS VAR. RECURVUS

ONE OF THE LAST DAFFODILS TO FLOWER IN THE SEASON, THE OLD PHEASANT'S EYE NARCISSUS HAS GORGEOUS, PURE WHITE NARROW PETALS AND A TINY YELLOW CENTRE WITH A RED-RIMMED EDGE TO IT. IT IS NOT ONLY SUBTLY BEAUTIFUL BUT ALSO DELICIOUSLY FRAGRANT.

You know spring has definitely arrived when the daffodils start to show their heads. Like a fanfare of floral trumpets heralding the start of the growing season, most commonly sold daffodils are loud, garish and brash. The majority are brightly coloured in egg-yolk yellow, with huge, almost iridescent petals and massive, elongated central trumpets in the middle of the flower, some of which are even frilly. That's not a bad thing and it certainly makes a statement in the garden or surrounding landscape.

However there are simply thousands of daffodils to choose from. Pheasant's eye is much more subtle than the common daffodil, straddling the middle ground between those narcissus that are almost so small, subdued and insignificant that you barely notice them, and the other, much bolder types. This daffodil still stands proud in the garden, but it feels as if it isn't showing off. Its beauty and confidence speaks for itself with its pure white flowers and the hypnotic 'eye' in its centre that catches yours, almost fixes you as you walk past. You can't help but stop and admire them.

It's a late-comer to the party also. Most daffodils have been and gone by the time this stunner arrives to grace the garden and there is a sense of calmness in the air, the gentle, soft lull before summer gets into full swing.

It's one of the aristocrats of the narcissus world and is one of the oldest in cultivation. Often called the poet's daffodil (partly because of the species name *poeticus*), it has throughout history inspired people to wax lyrical about it.

Peasant's eye requires full sun or partial shade and moist but well-drained soil. It has attractive, white windswept petals and tiny, red-rimmed yellow cups (the pheasant's eye) in the centre. It naturalises well in grass and mixes with snake's head fritillaries, primroses and cowslips in a wildflower mix.

ALTERNATIVES

N. 'Actaea' is very similar to pheasant's eye and is often sold as an alternative. It flowers a few weeks earlier.
Another subtle but beautiful narcissus is 'Thalia', which is pure white with slightly swept-back petals and a sweet fragrance.
I love *N. bulbocodium*, the tiny, low growing, hoop-petticoat narcissus with its quirky flower shape. It's like a funnel with tiny pointed petals. A real curiosity daffodil and a great talking point in the garden in early spring.
Another wonderful one to try is *N. cyclamineus* with its strongly swept-back petals. I always think that the yellow flowers look like lots of Bart Simpson heads on stems.

25 TULIP 'QUEEN OF NIGHT'

THERE IS NOTHING SO EXUBERANT AND FLAMBOYANT IN THE
GARDENING WORLD AS THE COMMON TULIP. THEY COME IN A RANGE
OF COLOURS AND SIZES PROVIDING A WELCOME SPLASH OF COLOUR
IN THE GARDEN EACH SPRING.

Tulips are usually grouped as goblet, bowl or cup shaped although there are more intricate forms too. In the seventeenth century the Dutch were gripped by Tulip Mania, a passion for buying up tulip bulbs for extraordinary prices, sometimes as much as the cost of a small house. Thankfully, bulbs are much cheaper now, and are now very much affordable.

Tulip 'Queen of Night' offers something a bit different to the traditional bright splash of colour. It offers a darker side, a contrast to the crazy colour combination of traditional tulip displays. The dark purple, almost black, cup-shaped flowers appear on single straight stems making it a great plant for the cut flower border.

Like most tulips they need a warm, sheltered site and require warm dry springs and a cold winter. Tulips prefer free-draining soil to prevent them rotting in the soil and developing fungal diseases so add plenty of grit or gravel into any heavy soil before planting. The bulbs should be planted in autumn before the arrival of hard frosts at a depth of three times the size of the bulb and about 10cm (4in) apart.

Tulips are perennial but most gardeners tend to treat the 'hybrid' types as annuals by digging them up after flowering and replanting the largest bulbs in autumn. Some gardeners use them like bedding and literally chuck them away and buy in new bulbs each autumn. The reason for this is that most hybrid tulips don't provide such a good display the following year. The type of bulbs known as 'species' are treated differently and remain in the ground from year to year.

Try doing a 50:50 mix with *Tulip* 'Ivory Floradale' for a simple but wonderful vanilla and chocolate colour combination.

ALTERNATIVES

An alternative dark tulip to 'Queen of Night' is a hybrid called 'Black Parrot' which has deep purple but twisted petals. For something a bit different try one of the wacky stripy varieties, such as 'Burning Heart' which has attractive creamy white flowers streaked with red. 'Burgundy Lace' is a graceful, glamorous tulip with beautiful deep red petals and fringed edges, while the variety 'Menton' is a classically-shaped tulip with pinkish red flowers with subtle orange hues.

PUTTING IT ALL TOGETHER

LARGE BORDER 6 M X 2 M

❶ Exochorda x macrantha 'The Bride'

❷ Magnolia stellata

❸ Corylus avellana 'Contorta'

❹ Clematis armandii

❺ Wisteria sinensis

❻ Euphorbia polychroma

❼ Erythronium 'Pagoda'

❽ Hyacinthoides non-scripta

❾ Pulmonaria 'Blue Ensign'

❿ Narcissus 'Pheasant's eye'

⓫ Viola tricolor

⓬ Vinca 'Dartington Star'

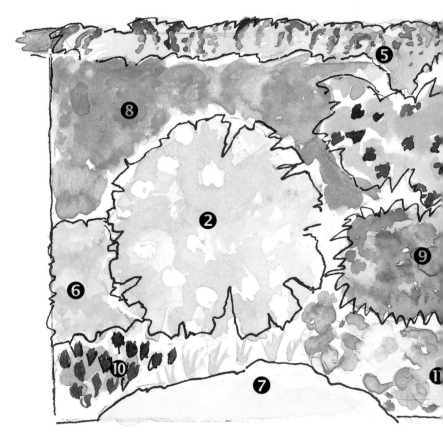

This is a typical spring mixed border, with a blue, yellow and white theme that will brighten up the early part of the year. The flowering canopies of the *Magnolia* and *Exochorda* are underplanted with classic spring ground cover plants, such as *Vinca* and *Pulmonaria*, carpeting the border with foliage and flowers, along with delightful spring bulbs. This border will thrive in full sun or part shade.

● Plant and train *Wisteria sinensis* to climb the back wall or fence in one direction and the *Clematis armandii* in the other.

● Plant *Exochorda x macrantha* 'The Bride' towards the back slightly off centre and the *Magnolia stellata* to the left but a little further towards the front. The third shrub *Corylus avellana* 'Contorta' which will provide showy catkins in spring as well as melodramatic structure can then be placed on the right hand side to complete the triangle.

WHATEVER SIZE YOUR SPACE, THERE IS A PERFECT WAY TO COMBINE
THE PLANTS IN THIS CHAPTER TO CREATE A PERFECT SPRING DISPLAY.
CHOOSE BETWEEN A DAZZLING DEEP BORDER, A TIDY CORNER OR
EVEN AN ISLAND BED.

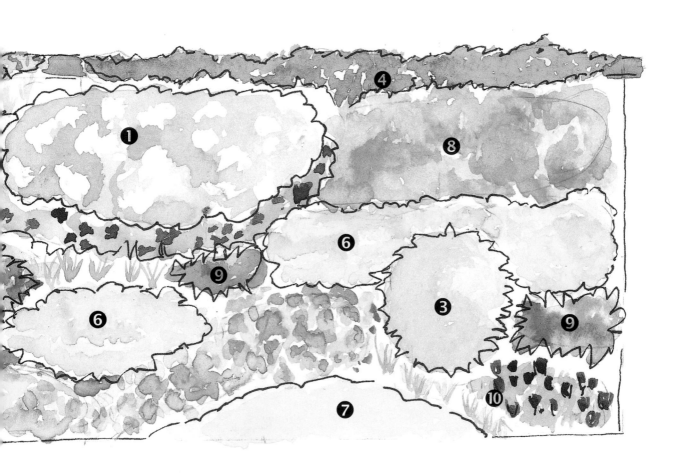

● *Hyacinthoides non-scripta*
and *Vinca* 'Dartington Star' can
be arranged in drifts along the
back. In front of these the bright
yellow *Euphorbia polychrome* and
Pulmonaria 'Blue Ensign' will
make a wonderful combination
and backdrop to the dainty
blooms of *Viola tricolour* and
Erythronium 'Pagoda', which
truly deserve their star position at
the front of the border.

Any gaps can be filled in with
natural drifts of *Narcissus*
'Pheasant's Eye' and for a later
splash of stronger colour, *Tulip*
'Queen of Night.'

A SPRING BORDER FOR SMALLER SPACES 5M^2

Perfect for a shaded corner this simple planting scheme will bring delicate colour and elegance to any garden. Avoid placing the camellia where it will get early morning sun, but otherwise all these plants need only a few hours sunlight each day to perform.

❶ Camellia williamsii 'Donation'
❷ Lamprocampsis spectabilis
❸ Aquilegia 'Nora Barlow'
❹ Fritillaria meleagris

● Plant *Camellia williamsii* 'Donation' at the back and a triangle of *Lamprocampsis spectabilis* in front, to show off its nodding, heart-shaped flowers. Fill any remaining gaps with natural drifts of *Aquilegia* 'Nora Barlow' and the delicate *Fritillaria meleagris*.

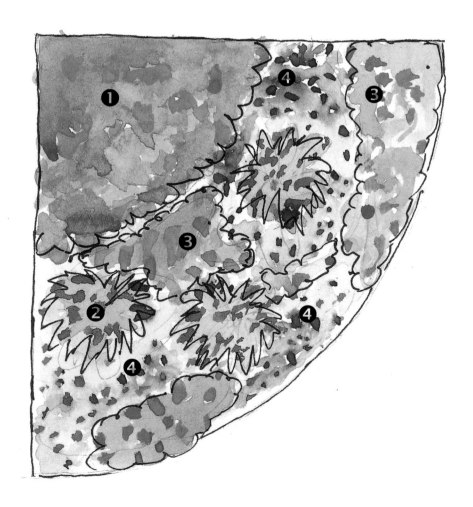

SPRING ISLAND BED 1-2 M DIAMETER

If space is limited this simple scheme will give the all the best spring has to offer without using up too much valuable space.

❶ Prunus 'Shogetsu'
❷ Mixed bulbs – Narcissus and Tulip

● Plant *Prunus* 'Shogetsu' in the centre of the bed for blossom in spring and autumn colour later on. Underplant with mixed bulbs such as *Narcissus* 'Pheasant's Eye' and *Tulip* 'Queen of Night', which will contrast well with the pure white cherry blossom.

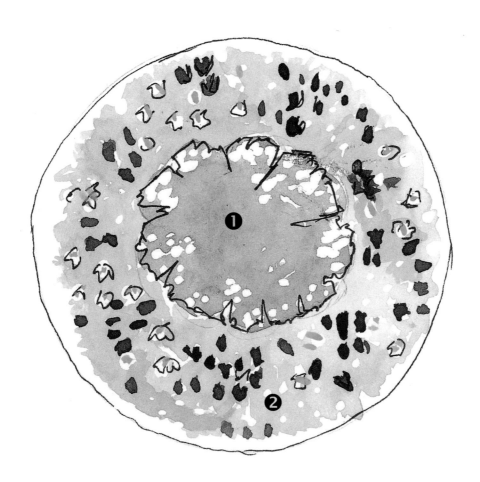

LOCATION, LOCATION, LOCATION

Probably the most important element of growing a plant successfully is placing it in the right location, with the correct amount of sunlight, suitable soil and ensuring it is hardy or tough enough to survive surrounding elements, such as frosts, prevailing winds and sea salt spray. Before running off to the garden centre to stock your garden full of plants, it is worth considering what conditions you have at home. Some plants, such as hawthorn are as tough as old boots and will tolerate anything nature will throw at them. Others are more refined and expect to be treated with respect. If you don't do this, they will either sit in the soil and sulk or, even worse, curl up and die.

ASPECT

Take time to study your garden and where the light falls. Look at it at different times of the day to see where the shadows and sunrays appear as the sun follows its trajectory during the course of the day, from rising in the east to setting in the west.

A garden facing south or south-west will receive the most amount of sun in the northern hemisphere. Of course, there are elements that can block the light such as a nearby building or large tree, but as a general rule of thumb, a south or south-west facing garden will be the warmest.

If the garden is on a south-west or south-facing slope then that is even better. This is why the best vineyards are always on south-facing slopes as they lie angled like solar panels maximising the sun's rays, enabling the grapes to ripen to their maximum. However, do be aware that the bottom of a slope can also be a frost pocket as the warm air rises and leaves the cold air below it. If there

is a hedge or wall at the bottom of the slope, this will prevent the cold air rolling away and traps it. So, avoid planting anything tender at the bottom of a slope.

South-west or south-facing walls are nearly always sun traps, making them ideal for plants that love it hot and dry.

North-facing gardens are often the shadiest as the sun often doesn't appear. However, there are loads of shade-loving plants, and many of them are maintenance free as they won't require the same amount of watering as those basking in the sun on the south side.

CHECKING YOUR SOIL

Once you've figured out how much sunlight your garden will receive, you also need to check the type of soil you have. Garden plants have all evolved from wild specimens, and many will still be quite particular about the conditions and crave an environment similar to their original habitat.

Firstly, check whether you have clay, loam or sandy soil. Clay soil is usually fertile but heavy, making it hard to dig. Unfortunately it tends to bake hard in the summer and get waterlogged in the winter due to its bad water-draining qualities. Sand is the opposite, usually being low in fertility and nutrients as it gets washed away too quickly. Plants tend to dry out quickly too as the sandy conditions are so free draining. The ideal soil for most plants is loam, as it combines the best of both clay and sand attributes, usually being fairly free draining but not so much that it can't retain nutrients. Of course, there are some plants that will like the extremes, so it's worth checking on the plant label as to what type of soil it prefers.

To check if you have clay or sandy soil

Take a sample of soil from the garden and try to roll it into a ball. If it does roll into a ball then it is clay. If it won't then it is sand.

Next try to roll it into a sausage shape. If it still holds its shape then it has a high clay content. If it breaks and crumbles then it is a loamy consistency.

Soil can be improved by adding organic matter into the ground, such as garden compost or rotted horse manure. The drainage of heavy clay soil can be improved by adding grit or sand.

Checking the pH of the soil

It is also important to check the acidic/alkaline levels of the soil as some plants are very sensitive to these. The most common examples are rhododendrons and camellias that require acidic soil. Soil testing kits can be bought, which will tell you what conditions you have, but another good way of telling what you have is to look at surrounding gardens. If you see lots of rhododendrons, camellias or heathers then it will tell you that the predominant soil in your area is acidic. If nobody is growing such plants then you can probably assume that the conditions aren't suitable. Of course is it still possible that you may have isolated pockets of acidic or alkaline conditions in your own garden, so if you're unsure then use a testing kit.

Opposite Before starting to plant it is important the soil is checked to see what plants will be suitable for growing in it.

Left Making sure you have the correct soil to suit the plant is essential before you start to sow any seeds.

BULB PLANTING

Bulbs are wonderful plants for brightening up most areas in the garden. Most are associated with flowering in spring, such as tulips, daffodils and crocus, but there are bulbs for all seasons. Technically, there are different types of 'bulbs', such as corms and tubers, but whatever their scientific category, they are all just basically underground sources of food and energy and are generally treated in exactly the same way. I've just categorised them all as 'bulbs' in this book to simplify things.

Do remember that very often bulbs need to be left to die down naturally after flowering, so avoid cutting back their foliage. This is worth considering when planting them, as their dying foliage can look scruffy if you've planted them as a centrepiece in your neat lawn or at the front of your border. Some top tips for planting bulbs:

Make sure that the bulbs are the right way up. Usually they have a pointed tip, which should face upwards towards the sky.

To get a naturalised effect, scatter the bulbs on the lawn and plant them where they fall, using either a trowel or a bulb planter.

When planting in a lawn add some leaf mould or general compost into each hole. Alternatively if planting in a flower bed, the entire area can be dug over first and compost added.

Most bulbs like moist but free-draining soil. If the soil is heavy, such as with high clay content, then the bulbs could rot in the ground. If this is the case, add a sprinkling of grit or horticultural sand into each hole with the bulb. There are a few exceptions, such as snake's head fritillaries, which thrive in damp, moist conditions.

Water the bulbs once planted if a dry spell is expected. Otherwise let the rain do the watering for you.

HOW DEEP TO PLANT THE BULB?

Most bulbs are usually planted at a depth of about two or three times their size. However, there are a few exceptions such as begonias which like to be near the surface, and tulips like to be quite deep.

Most spring and summer flowering bulbs are planted in autumn, such as daffodils, tulips, alliums. However there are few exceptions, such as dahlias, snowdrops, bluebells, gladioli and begonias, which are usually planted in spring. Bluebells and snowdrops are best planted 'in the green', when already in leaf.

Left Bulbs are an easy and cheap solution to providing lots of colourful interest in the garden in springtime.

Opposite left and right Check what planting depth is required for your bulbs prior to planting. Too deep and it may rot, too shallow and it could dry out.

Allium bulbs	10cm (4in) deep and 10cm (4in) apart	in full sun
Begonia bulbs	1cm (½in) deep and 30cm (12in) apart	in full sun or dappled shade
Crocus bulbs	10cm (4in) deep and 7cm (2½in) apart	in full sun or dappled shade
Daffodil bulbs	10cm (4in) deep and 10cm (4in) apart	in full sun or dappled shade
Dahlia bulbs	15cm (6in) deep and 45cm (18in) apart	in full sun
Bluebell bulbs	10cm (4in) deep and 10cm (4in) apart	in dappled shade
Hyacinth bulbs	10cm (4in) deep and 8cm (3in) apart	in full sun or dappled shade
Iris reticulata bulbs	10cm (4in) deep and 8cm (3in) apart	in full sun
Lily bulbs	20cm (8in) deep and 15cm (6in) apart	in full sun or dappled shade
Narcissus bulbs	10cm (4in) deep and 10cm (4in) apart	in full sun or dappled shade
Snowdrop bulbs	10cm (4in) deep and 10cm (4in) apart	in dappled shade
Tulip bulbs	15cm (6in) deep and 13cm (5in) apart	in full sun
Winter aconite bulbs	5cm (2in) deep and 5cm (2in) apart	in full sun or dappled shade

SUMMER

SUMMERTIME and the living is easy! The garden is at its fullest, overflowing with foliage and a cacophony of bright blooms. There is a wealth of interest and colour and a lavish richness of fragrances from all the flowers. As temperatures rise, many of the spring flowering shrubs and bulbs take a back step, and in the foreground and putting the sizzle into summer are predominantly the herbaceous perennials and the bedding plants.

Climbers such as wisteria, clematis, passionflowers, honeysuckles and scrambling roses begin their ascent towards the sky. Closer to the ground the herbaceous border provides an embarrassment of riches, ranging from alliums with their huge blue spheres held up high and jostling for position amongst other sizzling summer stalwarts creating a riot of colour, such as *Verbena bonarensis*, phlox, poppies, sea holly, lilies and geraniums.

Shrubs too provide not just colour but a sensory overload of scent as well with philadelphus, and of course the roses, with their heavenly scent catching on the warm summer breezes. Ceanothus create large blocks of deep blue colour, almost like floral walls, while fuchsias create a vivid brightness with their flowers hanging down from the stems, looking like ballerinas rejoicing and dancing because summer has arrived.

Summer is a time for getting outdoors, enjoying a barbeque or picnic on the lawn and soaking up those long, warm evenings. Often there is the distant, melodic throbbing of lawn mowers cutting grass, and the soporific buzz of bees dancing and bobbing around flowering plants such as lavender and rosemary.

As the warmth increases, it becomes a time for enjoying and relaxing in the garden, as much as physically doing the gardening. Pulling up a deck chair or lounger, slapping on the sun cream and relaxing with a good book and a cool drink, are just as much a part of summer gardening as cutting the grass and deadheading the roses. In larger gardens paddling pools are filled for children and badminton or croquet can be played on the lawn. If you have a small garden, summer is the perfect time to visit larger public gardens and open spaces to enjoy the ambiance, find some summer solace and enjoy the beauty of the surrounding world.

Previous page Paeonia lactiflora 'Bowl of Beauty'.

Left The Long Border at Snowshill Manor and Garden, Gloucestershire.

26 EUCRYPHIA X NYMANSENSIS 'NYMANSAY'

THIS IS POSSIBLY NOT THE EASIEST TREE TO FIND BUT WORTH SEARCHING OUT AS IT FLOWERS IN LATE SUMMER AND AUTUMN WHEN MOST OTHER TREES AND SHRUBS HAVE RIPENING BERRIES AND ARE CHANGING LEAF COLOUR.

Eucryphia originally come from the temperate rainforests of Australia and South America and so prefer a milder, wetter environment, such as the West Atlantic coast. On the whole they suit a woodland-style garden with slightly acidic soil. Put simply, if magnolias and rhododendrons are doing well in a planting scheme, eucryphia will too. Their flowers are adored by bees and make excellent honey.

It may be less well known than most ornamental trees but *Eucryphia* x *nymansensis* 'Nymansay' can be a superb addition to any medium-sized garden as long as it is placed properly. From August onwards it is festooned with white, four-petalled flowers and in mild areas will keep flowering for weeks and weeks. It is a wonderful sight to behold because it is so rare to come across trees flowering at this time of year.

To thrive it will require shelter from hard frost and cold north winds, preferably somewhere its roots are shaded but its leaves receive plenty of sunlight. A sheltered, south-facing hollow is ideal. A mulch of leaf mould around the base and underplanting with small- and medium-sized shrubs will help keep the roots cool and moist. Clay or sand are both suitable soils as long as the ground is moist but free draining.

Once suitably sited it can largely be left to its own devices. Rarely troubled by pests and not requiring any complicated pruning it should grow away merrily, eventually reaching over 12m (40ft) tall, although its spread will be considerably less.

ALTERNATIVES
This is a small group of plants so choice is limited but, if frost is an issue, you might consider trying *E.* x *intermedia*, bred for extra hardiness. It will require acidic soil, however.

27 CEANOTHUS X DELINEANUS 'GLOIRE DE VERSAILLES'

THERE IS NOTHING QUITE LIKE THE POWDER BLUE, FLUFFY FLOWERS OF THE CALIFORNIAN LILAC, AND IT WILL STAND OUT IN ALMOST ANY GARDEN SCHEME, GIVEN THE RIGHT KIND OF CONDITIONS.

With both evergreen and deciduous varieties available as well as spring flowering and late summer flowering types, the biggest difficulty is deciding which ceanothus would be most suitable. Some can grow over 6m (20ft) tall and are more like trees than shrubs. As a rule the evergreen types are the most sensitive to cold winds and frost, and will nearly always benefit from the protection of a south-facing wall, so a deciduous ceanothus may be more suitable in many cases.

Ceanothus x *delineanus* 'Gloire de Versailles' is the best of the deciduous types. It has a reputation for being the most tolerant of exposed conditions and is small enough at around 1.5m x 1.5m (5ft x 5ft) to fit nicely into an average garden, supplying delicate colour and fragrance towards the end of summer.

Like all ceanothus it dislikes sitting in wet, cold soil for any length of time so is best planted somewhere it can receive plenty of sunshine that will both warm up the ground and encourage flowering. A thick mulch of compost or manure will protect the roots from unfavourable conditions but do keep this away from the main stem to avoid rotting. These plants are ideal for gardens where the soil is slightly chalky and alkaline. However, on very chalky soils, especially shallow ones, they may suffer from chlorosis, where the leaves turn yellow between the veins as a result of nutrient deficiency.

As *C.* x *delineanus* 'Gloire de Versailles' flowers on new growth it should be trimmed in early to mid-spring to encourage lots of new flowering growth. Prune back the branches by about a half and remove any dead or frost-damaged wood that might be showing. Evergreen ceanothus on the other hand rarely recover from any real hard pruning so are best left alone or only gently trimmed.

ALTERNATIVES
C. thyrsifolius var. *repens* spreads a little wider rather than taller and is an excellent space filler, flowering in spring and early summer.

28 Syringa vulgaris 'Katherine Havemeyer'

BETWEEN THE EARLY DELIGHTS OF SPRING AND THE BOUNTEOUS WEALTH OF SUMMER COMES THE LILAC. ITS FRAGRANT, ROMANTIC BLOOMS IN PURPLE, PINK AND WHITE HAVE BEEN AROUND FOR CENTURIES, BUT BECAME POPULAR IN THE EARLY TWENTIETH CENTURY.

The common lilac has a number of cultivars and varieties for the modern gardener to choose from, including the classic *Syringa vulgaris* 'Katherine Havemeyer.' This medium-sized shrub grows to around 4m (13ft), initially upright but spreading with maturity. The heart-shaped leaves are mid-green and it produces neat, lavender-coloured panicles of double flowers in May, which age to lilac- pink, adding extra depth and tone. The flowers are deliciously fragrant.

All lilacs are hardy deciduous shrubs or trees, in the same family as the olive, and most will grow to a height of around 4 – 5m (13 – 16½ft). With age their trunks develop a pleasing, twisted and gnarled appearance. There are a number of smaller types available if space is limited.

Lilacs are easy to care for, unfussy plants as long as they receive plenty of sunshine and they are not sitting in waterlogged ground. Almost any type of soil, whether clay or sand, suits them. They are especially useful in areas of alkaline, chalky soil. As they originate from the rocky hills of the Balkans they tolerate exposure well and are superbly hardy. There is very little need to prune a lilac since its growth, although bushy, is naturally self-contained but some gardeners do choose to deadhead after flowering to ensure plenty of blooms the following year.

Lilacs are perfect in an informal planting scheme but their tolerance of drought means they can also be grown in large pots for a more formal effect.

ALTERNATIVES

S. vulgaris 'Alba' is pure white and adds classical elegance to any garden. If space is an issue try *S. pubescens* subsp. *microphylla* 'Superba', the Daphne lilac, a shrub that only grows 1.5m (5ft) high or the even smaller, slow growing *S. meyeri* 'Palubin'. Both produce smaller panicles of pink or purple flowers equally as fragrant as their bigger cousins.

29 PHILADELPHUS 'SYBILLE'

THE WHITE, BOWL-SHAPED BLOSSOM OF THE PHILADELPHUS SET
AGAINST DARK GREEN LEAVES IS AN IRRESISTIBLE COMBINATION, ONE
WHICH LOOKS AND SMELLS FABULOUS, ESPECIALLY ON LONG, BALMY
SUMMER EVENINGS.

Philadelphus, sometimes known as 'mock orange',
is a wonderful, early summer flowering shrub that
comes in a range of sizes suitable for almost any
garden space. Nearly all philadelphus are deliciously
scented and attractive to pollinators.

Of the many varieties available, *Philadelphus*
'Sybille' stands out for planting in a small- or
medium-sized garden. Growing to around 1.5m (5ft)
high and eventually spreading to 2m (6½ft) 'Sybille'
has a loose arching habit, with small, dark, toothed
leaves. From early June to mid-July it produces
white, open flowers with delicate brushstrokes of
purple in the centre. It is ideal for the front of a
shrub border or as a specimen in a small garden.

Philadelphus thrives in any situation where it
receives full sun or at least some sun for a large part
of the day. They appreciate moist but well-drained
soil, so do mulch well, but otherwise they tolerate
most soil types and garden aspects. They are able to
cope in coastal gardens, or in areas of high pollution.

As the flowers form on the previous year's stems,
these shrubs will require some simple pruning to
encourage new growth and plenty of flowers. Once
the flowers have finished in late July, cut out any
flowered growth back to a strong shoot below and
then remove a few of the older stems right back
down to ground level. The longer the philadelphus
has to grow during the summer, the better it will
flower the following year.

ALTERNATIVES
If you have the space for it at the back of
the border, *P.* 'Virginal' is a must with a
lemony scent and pure white double flowers,
where it will happily reach 3m (10ft). It is
also possible to grow a golden-leaved version,
P. coronaria 'Aurea', which needs siting away
from scorching, strong sunlight.

30 BUDDLEJA DAVIDII 'BLACK KNIGHT'

FORGET THE IMAGE OF BUDDLEJA AS A WEEDY SHRUB INFESTING RAILWAY BANKS AND TAKE A LOOK AT SOME OF THE MORE DRAMATIC, 'BUTTERFLY PLANTS' THAT WILL BE GREAT FOR WILDLIFE AND LOOK FANTASTIC IN THE LATTER PART OF THE SUMMER.

There are over a hundred species of nectar-rich buddleja from around the world, relished by a long list of pollinators that include humming birds in South America as well as butterflies closer to home. Although buddlejas are not native to Europe there are over 20 native species of butterflies that like to feast on these plants so they are an essential feature of any wildlife-friendly garden.

Buddleja davidii 'Black Knight' is a hardy shrub that, while vigorous, is unlikely to reach more than 4m (13ft) high. What marks it out from the 'railway' buddleja is the intense colour of its flowers. The small, compact spikes of dark purple make for a dramatic contrast to the silvery leaves. Flowers appear from late July through August but the season can be extended by regular deadheading.

In order to get the best out of any *B. davidii* a robust prune will be necessary once a year, in early spring. At this point all of the previous year's long woody growth and weak shoots should be cut back hard, to just one or two buds above the last cut. Without it they will quickly become long and leggy with a few flowers on their tips.

In almost every other way these are unfussy plants, tolerant of most soils as long as drainage is good and they can benefit from plenty of sunshine. They are drought resistant, so a great choice for difficult areas where other flowering shrubs would struggle.

ALTERNATIVES
B. davidii can be found in a range of colours, including white and pink if the intensity of *B. davidii* 'Black Knight' is too strong for a colour scheme. There are also some more unusual buddlejas that are worth searching out, such as *B. alternifolia*, a large, weeping shrub with a pale mauve flower and the fun *B. globosa* with its small orange pom poms.

31 ROSA 'DARCEY BUSSELL'

HOW COULD YOU CHOOSE A FAVOURITE FROM THE GREATEST AND BEST-LOVED FAMILY OF PLANTS EVER CULTIVATED? ROMANTIC, GOOD LOOKING AND SENSUALLY FRAGRANT, EACH ROSE HAS ITS OWN UNIQUE CHARACTERISTICS THAT SOMEONE HAS FALLEN IN LOVE WITH.

Perhaps it is not just the sheer beauty of the rose that makes it the best known, most admired flower in the garden. The glorious blooms of the rose are repositories of precious memories. The rose that climbed by the back door of Grandma's house, the anniversary present from a dear friend, the first rose we ever picked and gave to our childhood sweetheart, they intertwine with our lives in a way no other flower can. People have even died upholding the symbolic power of the rose.

If you have yet to form a relationship with a rose then you could begin with *Rosa* 'Darcey Bussell.' Like the dancer herself, this is a prima ballerina without any diva-like characteristics, a modern English shrub rose with an impeccable reputation and robust good health.

As it only reaches a height of little more than 1m (3ft) it is a perfect plant for the smaller garden, or for the front of a border. Siting it near a path or

patio is ideal to make the most of its fresh, fruity fragrance, one of its greatest charms. It can even be grown in a large pot if there is no other space for it.

The rich, deep red double blooms appear on this compact bush around the beginning of July and will continue to flower freely all summer long right into autumn. They have just the right amount of old-fashioned attraction for an informal cottage garden look but fit equally well, due to the strong colour, into more modern schemes.

All roses appreciate good, fertile, rich soil with enough moisture in order to do really well. Not all, however, require full sun, although *R*. 'Darcy Bussell' certainly prefers it. As to continuing care, rose pruning is a subject that fills up many pages of gardening manuals but *R*. 'Darcy Bussell' will simply require a light prune during the dormant period, like any other summer flowering shrub.

ALTERNATIVES

Roses that climb are a particular favourite of many people. Pillar roses such as *R*. 'New Dawn' will never overwhelm your garden so are good for smallish spaces. For a more natural effect *R. eglantina*, the rose mentioned by Shakespeare, is delightful. Scented single roses appear in midsummer, followed by small autumn hips. With few thorns this makes a superb hedge. Its whippy shoots can actually be woven together, providing extra interest even when bare in winter.

32 HEBE 'GREAT ORME'

MOST HEBES WOULD NOT STOP ANYONE IN THEIR TRACKS, BEING GOOD WORKADAY FILLERS IN THE SHRUB BORDER BUT HEBE 'GREAT ORME', AT LEAST, HAS FLOWER SPIKES THAT ARE IMPOSSIBLE NOT TO FALL IN LOVE WITH.

If you happen to live on the top of a cliff overlooking the sea, you may have the most wonderful view out of your windows, but finding plants that will cope with the exposure could be a real headache. Salt and wind are usually thoroughly disliked by many plants, blasting and scorching delicate leaves and blooms into oblivion.

Fortunately the hebe family is more than up to the task of surviving such harshness. In their home country of New Zealand hebes have developed tough leaves that shrug off salt and wind and are found colonising and thriving all over rocky, bare hillsides where little else grows. They are not always the most spectacular shrubs, but they are sturdy performers.

H. 'Great Orme' is, however, the one hebe that would fit in nicely in any border. The perfect size for a small garden, around 1.5m (5ft), it can provide excellent, all-round, evergreen structure with the added advantage of summer flower spikes of candy-pink that fade gently to white, reminiscent of coconut ice. Irresistible. As long as it is not exposed to long periods of frost or planted in acid soil it should thrive in sunshine with only the occasional minor prune.

ALTERNATIVES
Purple and white flowers are the most common colours in the hebe range, so if you find the pink too difficult to blend into your scheme, try a white variety such as *H. albicans* instead: smaller and more elegant but a little less tolerant of frost.

33 FUCHSIA 'MRS POPPLE'

IN LATE SPRING, NURSERIES DISPLAY ROWS OF OF FUCHSIAS TO ENTICE THE UNWARY. THESE ARE OFTEN TENDER SPECIES, FAR TOO DELICATE TO SURVIVE IN YOUR GARDEN ALL YEAR ROUND. THERE ARE GREAT FUCHSIAS, HOWEVER, THAT WILL STAND UP TO THE COLD OF WINTER.

Originally from South America, fuchsias were first discovered towards the end of the seventeenth century, but it took almost two hundred years for them to really 'arrive' here in Britain. Now it is impossible to count their numbers as breeding has created numerous hybrids and crosses.

For a fuchsia 'Mrs Popple' is practically a grand dame, one of the oldest and most reliably hardy of the group. The flowers are single, typically bright fuchsia-pink on the outside with a purple inner skirt inside protecting the long stamens. They are a good size for a hardy fuchsia.

One of the first fuschias to come into flower, often as early as June, it will reliably continue to flower until frost knocks it back. In mild areas such as the West Country, it may even continue flowering past Christmas, still putting out a few flowers while the daffodils are fattening up their own flower buds.

Pruning this sturdy, bushy plant is best left to spring when it is easier to see the results of any frost damage. To keep a relatively neat and compact shape, as this is a plant that likes to arch, it should be cut back hard, almost but not quite to the ground. It will not be too long before new growth appears. The hardy fuchsias are undemanding plants with few special requirements. They can even be grown in areas where there is only sun for part of the day. A few hours will be enough, useful if you have a city garden with shade-casting buildings nearby.

ALTERNATIVES
If space is limited 'Tom Thumb' is perhaps a better option. With small but profuse flowers it will form a low mound at the front of a border or in a rockery, ideal in a small garden. The species *F. microphylla* is also a suitable option, if you can find it, rarely growing more than 1m (3ft) tall with tiny, miniature flowers.

34 Lavendula angustifolia 'Hidcote'

ONE OF THE CLASSIC PLANTS OF THE TRADITIONAL ENGLISH GARDEN, LAVENDER IS INSTANTLY RECOGNISABLE AND LOVED BY ALL FOR ITS COLOUR AND FRAGRANCE, CONJURING UP BALMY SUMMER DAYS AND PICNICS ON THE LAWN.

It has been grown for centuries in herb and cottage gardens both for its Mediterranean good looks and as a useful herb. Historically, washing was often dried over lavender bushes to ensure fragrant and pest-free laundry and scented sachets of this herb are still a popular addition to wardrobes and closets.

Many lavenders are available, including white and pink versions, but *Lavendula angustifolia* 'Hidcote' is always a star performer.

Its bushy shape, silver grey-green foliage and dark, almost violet flowers are the most obvious of its charms, but this plant is also delightfully compact, growing no more than 1m (3ft) tall, and is hardier than many of its close relatives.

On the whole lavenders prefer basking in unlimited warm sunshine and poor, free-draining soil. They are most happy in chalky soils but will cope with neutral, even slightly acidic conditions as long as their roots are not sitting in the cold and the wet for too long. They are known to be drought tolerant so are great plants for a gravel garden or pot, preferably sited near a path so you can brush past it every day.

For gardens with heavier soil it is worth planting lavender on a mound, slightly above soil level, to prevent rotting in wet weather. Waiting until the sun has properly warmed the ground before planting out any variety of lavender is also a good idea.

To keep *L. angustifolia* 'Hidcote' from becoming woody at its base it needs to be pruned yearly. In late summer trim off the old flowers completely and cut back the growth by a couple of centimetres. A second pruning for an even tighter effect can be done in early spring, cutting the whole plant back to the most compact shape you can manage. A football-shaped bush will ensure next year's flowers appear all over and not just at the top, but cutting back to bare, woody stems should be avoided as the plant is unlikely to recover.

ALTERNATIVES

For a more informal effect *L. angustifolia*, the true English lavender, will provide a bigger, looser plant with longer flower spikes in a paler tone. Or try one of the French lavenders, *L. stoechas*, with its cheeky ears, in a sheltered, south-facing spot. If you can find it, the deciduous azalea *Rhododendron* 'Greenway', named after Agatha Christie's holiday home with its woodland garden in Devon, is worth growing. It is a small, low growing evergreen shrub producing masses of funnel-shaped, pink flowers.

35 CISTUS 'JESSAMY BEAUTY'

THE PERFECT PLANT TO GIVE YOUR PATIO OR GARDEN A
MEDITERRANEAN FLAVOUR, CISTUS, OR ROCK ROSE, IS MORE USED
TO THE HEAT OF MOROCCO AND THE CANARIES BUT SHOULD BE
PERFECTLY HAPPY IN ANY HOT, SHELTERED SPOT YOU CAN PROVIDE.

An evergreen plant from around the Mediterranean
Sea, cistus flowers constantly throughout summer
into early autumn but, unusually, each of its tissue
paper flowers only lasts one day. You will find them
opening just after sunrise but by around 4pm every
one of the multitude of petals will have dropped to
the ground, only to be replaced overnight by new
buds just waiting their turn to sunbathe.

These are really plants for poor soil. Acid or alkaline
matters very little but it does need to be free
draining. Wet roots will only cause rotting. Sunny,
sheltered banks and slopes would suit them best, or
a sheltered and warm patio, although you may not
appreciate the constant petal drop in this case.

Of the many hybrids available 'Jessamy Beauty' is a
favourite. Fast growing and hardier than many, this
has white, paper-thin petals with red markings near
the centre.

ALTERNATIVES
The pink flowers of other hybrids like *C.* x
pulverulentus look lovely set against their
greyish, muted leaves.

36 ERYNGIUM ALPINUM

AMONGST ALL THE FROTH AND FRILLS OF THE SUMMER BORDER THERE
IS ALWAYS ROOM FOR A LITTLE BIT OF EDGINESS AND ERYNGIUM
ALPINUM, ONE OF THE SEA HOLLIES, IS THE PERFECT PLANT TO ADD
JUST SUCH AN ELEMENT.

There is nothing quite like the super metallic blue vibrancy of the eryngiums. From a low growing rosette of glossy foliage these spiky flowerheads appear like magic in midsummer. The actual flowers are the blue cones in the centre, surrounded by softly spiny, feathery bracts that make the flowerheads look as if they have been breathed upon by Jack Frost. Amongst a cloud of gypsophilia or partnered with a pale yellow day lily they look simply fantastic. Even when faded they keep their shape throughout autumn, providing extra interest right until they absolutely have to be cut back. They will also self-seed, giving you lots of new plants the following spring.

Despite its common name of sea holly, *Eryngium alpinum* comes from the alpine mountains of Switzerland, rather than from the seaside. It is however extremely hardy as a result and still suits coastal gardens very well.

ALTERNATIVES

The biggest and most silvery of the eryngiums, *E. giganteum*, is truly dramatic. Known as 'Miss Wilmott's Ghost', after the rather redoubtable Victorian lady who took it upon herself to scatter seeds in gardens that she visited, its stature and presence is awe-inspiring. Not one for the faint-hearted.

37 PAEONIA LACTIFLORA 'BOWL OF BEAUTY'

PEONY FLOWERS ARE REAL SHOWSTOPPERS. THEY CAN BE HUGE AND ALWAYS LOOK SO PERFECTLY FORMED. PEONIES ORIGINATE FROM CHINA AND JAPAN AND IT IS NO SURPRISE THAT THEY APPEAR IN SO MUCH OF THEIR MYTHOLOGY AND ORIENTAL ART.

If you want an herbaceous perennial with the wow factor then the peony is it! Some peonies can be huge, measuring over 30cm (12in) in diameter and they come in a huge range of colours and shapes including single, double and the anemone.

Paeonia 'Bowl of Beauty' is one of the most commonly grown peonies with massive, deep pink, bowl-shaped flowers with a cluster of deep cream in its centre. It is an anemone type of peony and the name 'Bowl of Beauty' couldn't describe this stunning flower any better. It also has a heavenly fragrance. The leaves are an attractive feature of this clump-forming perennial with lots of mini leaflets. Peonies can either be grown in a spring flowering border or a cottage garden. In some grander gardens there are actual specific beds dedicated to growing just peonies.

They do have an unfair image of being difficult to grow, but a few tricks should ensure their success. The key rule to ensuring the survival of your peony is to not plant it too deeply as they are so susceptible to rotting. Plant the crown literally just below the surface in moist, fertile and free-draining soil. Peonies don't respond well to being disturbed either so make sure you are definitely happy with its position before putting it into the ground. If you do have to move a peony then don't be surprised if it doesn't flower for a year or two after transporting. Prior to planting, prepare the ground well to ensure any hard pans are broken up and add plenty of well-rotted organic matter. Due to the weight of the flowerheads, staking is usually essential unless there are other surrounding plants close by that can prop it up. Get the structure of the stakes in early, as the flowers are fragile and disintegrate easily if they're being moved about.

Peonies like a warm, sunny site but avoid exposed sites because the flowers will quickly be destroyed by the wind and driving rain. Cut foliage back in autumn as soon as it starts to die back to avoid problems with peony wilt.

ALTERNATIVES

P. mlokosewitschii, affectionately known by gardeners as 'Molly the witch', is one of the easier peonies to grow, being tolerant of a wider range of soils and not so likely to sulk in less favourable conditions. It produces masses of large, lemon-coloured flowers. It's the perfect plant for the front of an herbaceous border, reaching only about 40cm (16in) high, providing early spring colour.

P. officinalis 'Rubra Plena' is an attractive and popular peony, with dark green, divided leaves and fully rich crimson flowers that get up to 20cm (8in) across.

P. lactifolia 'Sarah Bernhardt' is another popular peony, reaching up to 90cm (nearly 3ft) in height, with attractive divided foliage and fragrant, rose-pink double flowers, with ruffled inner petals.

38

DELPHINIUM ELATUM

THE TOWERING SPIKES OF A WELL-MAINTAINED DELPHINIUM ARE A TRUE HIGHLIGHT OF THE CLASSIC ENGLISH HERBACEOUS BORDER AND TO PICK A PARTICULAR FAVOURITE FROM THOSE AVAILABLE IS ALMOST IMPOSSIBLE. THEY ARE ALL SIMPLY WONDERFUL.

If there is one name more associated with the delphinium than any other, it has to be that of the doyenne of English garden design, Gertrude Jekyll. Her painter's mastery of form and colour harmonies were second to none and anyone aspiring to achieve a similar, subtle, glorious informality in their own garden should definitely be looking to plant a delphinium or two to make the most of their structure and colour range. Combine them with lavender, campanula and oriental poppies and you have all the main ingredients for an Arts and Crafts inspired border.

In a way delphiniums are the archetypal herbaceous perennial. They require some effort to grow successfully, not least because slugs and snails adore them, and a combination of good, loamy, fertile soil, sunshine and temperate weather. On top of this they will usually require staking and thinning out to look their best. However, if looked after properly, the flowers are a rich and ample reward for all your travails. Their star may only shine briefly but it shines with a light that is simply dazzling.

Delphinium elatum has parented many new delphiniums in a fantastic range of colours, from deep purple to white with almost every shade between. The blue colour palette is especially exciting. Paler blue delphiniums such as 'Centurion Sky Blue' have a dream-like quality about them that fits well in pastel designs, reflecting hazy summer skies, while the brighter blues bring freshness and vibrancy. 'Blue Nile' is a perfect example of a mid-blue delphinium that mixes well with sunny yellow colours, giving any garden a bit of zing.

The *elatum* hybrids are the tallest of the family, the dense flower spikes rising to 1.5m (5ft) above their leaf rosettes. Removing these spikes as soon as they have flowered in early summer often means a repeat performance later in the season.

ALTERNATIVES
Outside of the blue delphinium there are numerous other great hybrids to choose from. *D.* 'Black Knight' has a dense, deep violet flower, *D.* 'Tiddles' is a more delicate grey-mauve and the best of the whites is usually considered to be *D.* 'Elizabeth Cook'.

39

GERANIUM
'JOHNSON'S BLUE'

NOT EVERY PLANT IN THE BORDER CAN BE A PRIMA DONNA. THE STAR OF ANY OPERA IS ALWAYS SUPPORTED BY A CHORUS THAT HELPS TO MAKE HER SHINE. HARDY GERANIUMS MAY BE BACKGROUND PERFORMERS BUT THEIR SUPPORTING ROLE IS ESSENTIAL.

In many ways the hardy geranium is a gardener's best friend. Without doubt they are the most popular herbaceous plants around, appreciated for their ease of care and durability. Never to be confused with the bedding plant, though still often referred to by the same name despite all attempts to rename it, most true geraniums, despite their tough reputation, are harmonious and gentle fillers that offer a respite from bigger, showier plants. They are excellent for repeating across the border to link disparate elements together.

There are geraniums available that provide flowers from late spring right the way through to late autumn but those of the summer border are probably the best looking of all of them. *Geranium* 'Johnson's Blue' is a favourite, loved both for its well-behaved mound of almost tripartate leaves as well as its bright blue flowers. The leaves themselves are fairly dark, picking up and emphasising the deep violet veining of the flowers wonderfully.

All hardy geraniums are extremely easy to look after. They are utterly hardy and pretty indifferent to the conditions they are grown in. Chalk, sand, clay or silt, sun or dappled shade; as long as they have some access to moisture they will merrily flower away for you without demanding too much attention. Having said that they will flower even more profusely than ever if you do give them better conditions but their performance, even if neglected, is still excellent. In mid- to late summer the first flush of flowers can be sheared off to encourage a second round of flowering and sometimes even a third if autumn is mild.

ALTERNATIVES
White-flowered geraniums are often very useful as they seem to retain their clear colour well. The leaves and growth of *G. clarkeii* 'Kashmir White' are smaller and more delicate but will shine bright in part shade. For even more delicacy try *G. phaeum*, the mourning widow, which has deep, almost black flowers, held about 15cm (6in) above the marked leaves. Small but perfectly formed.

There are a number of blue flowering hyacinths available, but *Hyacinthus orientalis* 'Blue Jacket' has one of the best fragrances. If you don't have room in the garden they can be grown in window boxes where you will get a wonderful whiff of these bright blue flowers every time you open the window.

40 VERBENA BONARIENSIS

CLOUDS OF PURPLE VERBENA BONARIENSIS RISING THROUGH GRASS DRIFTS ARE ONE OF THE MOST RECOGNISABLE CHARACTERISTICS OF WHAT IS KNOWN AS PRAIRIE GARDENING AND SIMILAR PRINCIPLES WILL ENHANCE YOUR BORDERS IN MUCH THE SAME WAY.

Verbena bonariensis is the tallest member of the *Verbena* family, with multiple stems that rise over 1.5m (5ft) into the air. Its small plates of purple flowers are attractive to pollinators and are long lasting. In fact *V. bonariensis* should flower from July all the way through to November with little attention. The long, thin stems can easily snap hence they are nearly always planted amongst thicker, sturdier plants that will protect them from breakage. Fortunately, the lightness and airiness of their flowerheads means that they can rise above almost any type of plant without cutting out light, offering a cloud-like extra layer that always seems to soften and naturalise any planting scheme. They are excellent plants for linking disparate elements of your design together, connecting without intruding, especially as they will self-seed themselves.

As a rule they prefer sandy and neutral soil as well as full sun so are not suitable for damp, shady spots and despite being officially perennial they are often very short lived. It is usually best to leave the cutting back of the stems until spring, which is no hardship as the stems and stalks stand up well through the chill of winter and, of course, this should ensure that the seeds spread far and wide in case the original plant does not make it. It is also possible to plant them in groups in sheltered areas to provide an airy, feathery foil to more substantial groups of plants.

ALTERNATIVES

V. hastata has pink to purple flowers and more of a structural feel to it, with a candelabra-effect flower spike while there are a whole plethora of verbena that can be grown as annuals, either at the front of the border or in pots and hanging baskets. *V.* 'Sissinghurst' is probably the best known of these.

41

NEPETA 'SIX HILLS GIANT'

THE AROMATIC LEAVES OF CATMINT HAVE A CERTAIN REPUTATION AMONGST CAT OWNERS BUT NEPETA 'SIX HILLS GIANT' IS A GARDEN HYBRID THAT WAS BRED TO MAKE HUMANS NOT CATS HAPPY AND WILL GRACE ANY BORDER WITH ITS SOFT PRESENCE.

If the pruning of lavender does not appeal to you, or you have soil too heavy for lavender to thrive, *N.* 'Six Hills Giant' should be right up your street. Although a member of the nettle family, it makes an excellent substitute plant: unfussy, drought resistant and easy to care for. The grey-green leaves, the aromatic fragrance and the lavender blue flower spikes can be used wherever lavender would look good, with much less fuss. It makes an excellent underplanting for roses, helping to deter aphids and covering the bare ground in between without over-competing for nutrients.

If you shear off the first flush of flower stalks after they have gone over you will nearly always get a second flush before autumn sets in. Eventually though you will need to chop the whole plant right back like any other herbaceous perennial.

For those worried that they may attract more unwelcome cats into the garden by planting this, be reassured that it seems to be only the true catmint *N. cataria* that has a euphoric effect.

ALTERNATIVES

If you do wish to make your own cat happy planting *N. cataria*, the source of catnip, is worth considering. It is a much smaller plant but its impact on your feline friend is definitely worth watching, while doing no real harm. A warning though, humans who try to eat catnip are reputed to become aggressive rather than euphoric, so leave it to Kitty.

42

CAMPANULA LACTIFLORA

IT IS HARD TO RESIST THE BELLFLOWER FAMILY WITH THEIR THIMBLE-SHAPED FLOWERS AND EASY-GOING HABIT. SMALLER ONES MAKE FOR WONDERFUL ROCKERY PLANTS BUT THE REAL STARS ARE THE TALLER, BRANCHING HERBACEOUS PERENNIALS OF THE SUMMER BORDER.

With erect, many branched stems, *Campanula lactiflora* is a reliable and effective choice for a summer border. At around 75cm (30in) high it can fit nicely at the back of a small border or be planted in delightful drifts through the middle of a more substantial space. They have a natural casualness, which suits relaxed planting schemes that include old-fashioned roses and other cottage garden flowers in the mix, especially if not staked as they will become a little lax as the season wears on. If the laxity bothers you then give them a framework of support at the start of the growing season to keep them in check.

The spires of cup-shaped flowers in shades of blue, lavender, pink or white are held above attractively pointed leaves for a surprisingly long time. Deadheading promptly should encourage a second flush later on and will stop the plant self-seeding.

Although they need plenty of sunshine, the intensity of the blue varieties will fade a little in full sun so are best planted where a little shade is available during the hottest part of the day. Other than this they have the same needs as most herbaceous perennials; fertile, moisture retentive soil that is neither too chalky nor too acidic.

ALTERNATIVES

C. lactiflora 'Lodden Anna' is a reliably pink bellflower with similar characteristics to its parent. For something a little more unusual search out *C. punctata*. These are compact plants whose tighter narrow bells hang down with just the smallest of flaring at the end. Lovely for the front of the border.

43 PHLOX PANICULATA 'BRIGHT EYES'

AT THE END OF A WARM, SUNNY SUMMER'S DAY NOTHING COULD BE BETTER THAN A COMFORTABLE GARDEN CHAIR, A GLASS OF SOMETHING OR OTHER AND THE PERFUME OF PHLOX. PURE HEAVEN.

Phlox looks as if it should flower at the beginning of summer not towards the end. Indeed, perhaps that is one of its charms, continuing the English cottage garden style right until the moment autumn shows up. Its delicate scent, at its best in the evening, also makes it a star performer so try and plant it where it can be appreciated.

Originally from North America, where it naturally can make a very tall plant, most modern phlox has been bred for compactness to avoid the need for extra support. If you do like the flowers of a taller variety this is a plant that responds well to the 'Chelsea chop' (roughly during the time of the RHS Chelsea Flower Show). Cut back by half in May and you will create a bushier, sturdier plant that still flowers with wild abandon.

With flower domes that range in colour from white, though carmine red to lilac and violet, there is bound to be a plant to suit your garden. *Phlox paniculata* 'Bright Eyes' is especially lovely with a delicate pink colour and conspicuous purple markings towards the centre.

Phlox do not like conditions to be too dry so plant in good, fertile soil with plenty of organic matter to hold on to any moisture. They are also surprisingly shade tolerant and will be fine with around four hours of sun a day, which makes them excellent choices for planting near a wall or fence.

ALTERNATIVES
There are some variegated phlox available, the most successful of which is *P. paniculata* 'Norah Leigh'. With cream variegated leaves and baby pink flowers this is one of those plants that you will either love or hate. For small spaces *P. subulata*, which is mat forming and slow spreading, makes an excellent edging plant.

44 PAPAVER ORIENTALE 'PATTY'S PLUM'

THIS EARLY SUMMER PERENNIAL IS THE MOST INCREDIBLE SHADE OF DEEP MAGENTA AND IS HEART-STOPPINGLY BEAUTIFUL. FOR A SHORT WHILE IT WILL BE THE ENVY OF ALL WHO SEE IT AND YOU WILL BE PLAGUED BY REQUESTS FOR ITS NAME.

The oriental poppies come from the near rather than the far east as their name would suggest and they do best in sandy, free-draining soil. They are usually some of the earliest of the great summer perennials to begin flowering, in May, and some of the earliest to finish unless you take action.

The delicate tissue flowers of the oriental poppy can be simple, ruffled and creased or even sometimes fringed, and come in a fantastic range of colours, many with dark spots and smudges that give them a rather painterly look. The secret of extending their flowering is to deadhead the flowers before they have a chance to fill their pepper pot seedheads, although in the case of *Papaver orientale* 'Patty's Plum' the seedpods themselves are almost as lovely as the flowers, the top being crowned with magenta velvet.

As soon as the last flower has faded the whole plant can be cut almost to the ground. This puts paid to the ugly decay of the dying leaves and may even

encourage a second flush of blooms later in the season. Plant something late flowering nearby to hide the gap.

ALTERNATIVES
P. orientale 'Mrs Perry' is one of the oldest selections available, in a delicate salmon-pink. For drama *P. orientale* 'Black and White' with ruffled petals and black smudges is hard to beat.

45

IRIS SIBIRICA

IT MAY SEEM SURPRISING TO PREFER IRIS SIBIRICA TO THE VAST SELECTION OF BEARDED IRISES, BUT WHAT MAKES A GOOD PLANT IS NOT ALWAYS JUST A MATTER OF OBVIOUS BEAUTY. GOOD MANNERS CAN BE EQUALLY IMPORTANT.

Iris sibirica is much better behaved than its gaudy cousins, like the quiet, thoughtful heroine of a Jane Austen novel rather than one of the frivolous, shallow characters that populate her Georgian salons and drawing rooms. Although it has rhizomes, the narrow, upright leaves are taller and more grass-like, making a manageable clump that can be divided only if you need more plants or otherwise left to its own devices. The flowers of the Siberian flag are cleaner and more refined, usually in shades of violet blue with classic iris markings. They appear from late May onwards through the entirety of June before producing seedheads that are interesting in their own right. Both the leaves and the seedpods can be left for the rest of the summer to provide structure before being cut down with other herbaceous perennials.

Although the common name for *I. sibirica* is bog iris, wet conditions are not essential. It does prefer moist soil and makes an excellent riverbank marginal but can be successfully grown in almost any garden as long as some extra organic matter is added at planting time. Otherwise it is very easy-going.

ALTERNATIVES
I. chrysographes is a favourite of designers. Fairly small, although still grouped with other Siberian irises, what makes it special is its dark purple, almost black flower. Very striking.

46

CROCOSMIA 'LUCIFER'

CROCOSMIA 'LUCIFER' IS GUARANTEED TO BRING A SPLASH OF VIVID COLOUR TO YOUR BORDER, HERALDING THE START OF THE SUMMER SEASON'S HOT COLOURS WHILE NEEDING VERY LITTLE ATTENTION.

Despite its South African origins, crocosmia is thoroughly at home in the northern hemisphere. So much so that along the lanes of Devon and Cornwall each summer, the orange spikes of montbretia, its older name, now outcompete many of our native plants to brighten up our journeys. Having escaped long ago from the garden environment they are now pretty well naturalised.

The flowers of *C*. 'Lucifer' come a little earlier than normal but their scarlet red is visually striking. Each individual bulb in a clump will produce a flower spike around 1.5m (5ft) above the ground, while the sword-like leaves are narrow, slightly pleated and a fresh bright green colour to set off the flowers perfectly.

Crocosmia do love a good summer shower but as long as they are in full sun and good soil they will be happy and require little in the way of the gardener's attention.

ALTERNATIVES
While *C*. 'Lucifer' makes a bold statement, other members of the family are surprisingly subtle so if this is your preference look for *C*. x *crocosmifolia* 'Norwich Canary' or 'Lady Hamilton', which are both apricot coloured and a little smaller.

47 ALLIUM 'GLOBEMASTER'

THE PERFECTLY ROUND BALLS OF ORNAMENTAL ALLIUMS, HELD ALOFT
ABOVE STRAPPY GREEN FOLIAGE, ADD A REAL TOUCH OF SCULPTURAL
GLAMOUR TO ANY HERBACEOUS BORDER IN EARLY SUMMER.

Closely related to the humble onion, alliums look
like balloons rising up from the greenery below. It
is hard to imagine that their thin stalks could have
the strength to hold up the spherical flowerheads
but they somehow seem to stand up tall and proud,
demanding to be seen and admired.

Allium 'Globemaster' with its crystal blue fortune-
teller's ball shape is one of the most impressive
varieties available. Flowering reliably through June
and July., it looks amazing dotted within a border,
especially before the majority of other herbaceous
plants have started to flower. Planting them this way
also helps to disguise any decaying leaves, which
occasionally do start to yellow before the end of
the flowering period. It is possible to plant them *en
masse* for an outstanding display, but you would then
need to think about plants to precede and follow
them as otherwise you will be left with bare ground
for much of the year.

All alliums like sunny, open and well-drained
conditions. In exposed, cold or waterlogged sites,
the dormant bulbs will rot far too easily. Adding
grit to heavy soils or removing the bulbs each year
to a drier position can also be tried, but it is far
better to site them in the right place from the start.

The flowerheads are a magnet for bumble bees and
other pollinators and dry well so can be left until
the end of summer to delight onlookers with their
filigree sculptural forms.

ALTERNATIVES
Smaller and more egg shaped, *A.
sphaerocephalon* flowers later in the season
and is best planted in small groups for best
effect. It is a good choice around roses where
the onion aroma may help to ward off pests.

48

Lilium candidum

THE PUREST OF THE PURE, LILIUM CANDIDUM, THE MADONNA LILY, IS SIMPLY THE FINEST, MOST ELEGANT LILY AROUND, THE CLARITY OF COLOUR AND DELICIOUS FRAGRANCE MAKING OTHER LILIES SEEM GAUDY IN COMPARISON.

Not for nothing has this glorious bulb long been associated with the Virgin Mary. Come summer the flowering stems of *Lilium candidum* will produce anywhere from 5–20 trumpet blooms, and a heady perfume that becomes ever more intense as the sun warms up. They usually grow anywhere from 1–2m (3–6½ft) high, just right for the middle of the border or a large pot.

Lilies are especially good at living in pots and actually seem to do better than they would in the ground. It is always worth having a few spare pots of lilies around in early summer as they can easily be dropped into bare patches in the border or spaces where a spring flowering plant has died back. Whether you dig a hole and plant them, pot and all, or simply hide the offending pot behind another suitably dense plant is up to you. If you have very heavy soil then the latter is probably the only option available, since lilies prefer light, well-drained, chalky soil to heavier, moister clays and silts where the bulbs may rot, especially during winter's dormancy. Once the flowering season is over the pots can then be removed and stored in a frost-free environment until spring arrives once more.

If lilies are planted directly into the ground to be left through the winter then it is probably advisable to add sand to the bottom of the planting hole as well as organic matter to improve drainage and the chances of rotting. Keeping an eye out for slugs and snails, which adore young lily shoots, is also essential.

ALTERNATIVES

With so many varieties available it is hard to pick out the best. The Asiatic lilies, especially, come in a wide range of colours and patterns and are relatively inexpensive. *L.* 'Stargazer' is a good example, with red petals, spotted with purple and edged in white. You could also try *L. superbum*, the Turk's cap lily, for a touch of eastern mysticism, especially in areas that do not receive a full day's sun.

49

CLEMATIS 'JACKMANII'

WITH A VAST RANGE OF SPECIES THERE IS BOUND TO BE A CLEMATIS TO SUIT EVERY TASTE. THE SUMMER FLOWERING CLEMATIS ARE NOT JUST BIG AND BOLD, THERE ARE ALSO VARIETIES WITH EXQUISITE BELLS, DELICATE PASTEL SHADES OR RICH VELVET TONES.

Clematis 'Jackmanii' is reliably hardy, long flowering and relatively easy to care for. It looks beautiful trained on a trellis against a wall or fence or will vigorously twine amongst your shrubs and trees, reaching a height of 3–4m (10–13ft) and covering any flowering gaps you may have as a result of spring's fleeting flourish. The flowers are big but elegant, velvety purple star shapes that are freely produced along the stems and side-shoots throughout the summer.

It is now standard practice to make sure that the roots of any clematis are kept cool, by shading with low growing plants or mulching with a thickish layer of pebbles to avoid the dreaded clematis wilt, but apart from this clematis will perform in most soil types with reasonable fertility, slightly more so on chalk. They can be planted a little below pot level to encourage plenty of new shoots to form from the base but this is not essential.

What puts people off growing clematis are the seemingly complicated instructions on pruning. This is really only a consequence of the sheer variety in the clematis family, especially as there always seems to be one kind or another in flower no matter the time of year. The summer flowering clematis are usually from one of two groups. Some flower early on small new growth and are pruned much more lightly in spring. C. 'Jackmanii' is in the later flowering group so its long season's growth has to be cut back harder the following spring with all older stems pruned back to a new strong bud that is just about to unfurl.

Mixing different clematis together in harmony or contrast works very well, as these deciduous plants are rarely so leafy that they compete with each other.

ALTERNATIVES
For the most showy, glamorous clematis flower try something like C. 'Ruby Wedding' or C. 'Nelly Moser.' At the other end of the scale the delightful C. 'Gravetye Beauty' bears a wealth of red flowers that are shaped like tiny, lily-flowered tulips.

50 LONICERA PERICLYMENUM 'BELGICA'

LOVED BY COUNTLESS GENERATIONS OF GARDENERS, ENJOYED BY
BEES AND CHILDREN LOOKING FOR A FREE SWEET TREAT AND EVEN
MENTIONED IN SHAKESPEARE, THE HONEYSUCKLE IS AS ENGLISH AS
HIGH TEA AND BUTTERCUPS AND DAISIES.

It is still possible to find our native honeysuckle,
Lonicera periclymenum, scrambling through
hedgerows and thickets in the wild, but for the
garden there are numerous other varieties available
bred to suit the gardener's needs.

L. periclymenum 'Belgica' is equally as fragrant as
the common honeysuckle but flowers just that little
bit earlier. It, too, is a fairly vigorous scrambler that
can equally be used to cover a wall or left to make
its way up through a host shrub or tree, to provide
early summer colour. The glorious scent is strongest
at night so it is wonderful to plant outside a house
window where the heady, sensual perfume will drift
in on warm evenings.

L. periclymenum 'Belgica's raspberry and cream
coloured flowers will gently fade with age before
producing berries that are a magnet for birds in
autumn but should not be eaten by humans. The
plant flourishes best when its roots are shaded so do
not try to grow it in full sunlight. Shade for part or
even most of the day will suit it much better.

ALTERNATIVES
For a later flowering plant *L. periclymenum*
'Serotina' can't be beaten. There are also
some wonderful, yellow-flowered forms
available such as *L. periclymenum* 'Graham
Thomas', which are cool and elegant.

51

PASSIFLORA CAERULAE

FOR A TOUCH OF THE TRULY EXOTIC WITHOUT TOO MUCH EFFORT, TRY GROWING THE PASSIONFLOWER AGAINST A SOUTH-FACING FENCE OR WALL WHERE YOU CAN ENJOY THE BIZARRE-LOOKING FLOWERS AND SHINY ORANGE FRUIT, THOUGH THIS IS NOT THE EDIBLE VARIETY.

Despite its South American origins, the passionflower can be grown quite successfully in Britain, given a little bit of consideration for its background. It is a strong, usually evergreen climber that holds on to its support with wiry tendrils. The shiny, finger-like leaves provide a good backdrop to the unusual flowers, which are white petalled, with an inner purple fringe and very prominent and sculptural centres that look a little like gyroscopic helicopters.

The name 'passionflower' has an interesting history. The early Christian missionaries used the flower to teach the indigenous population of South America about their faith, with each part of the flower representing an important aspect of Christ's life.

If cold winters are a problem it is better grown in a pot and overwintered but otherwise giving it as much shelter, warmth and sun as you can manage should keep it happy. It is a perfect specimen for a city courtyard, for example, as long as it is not too shaded. Otherwise it is undemanding, tolerating most soils and needing only average fertility and water.

ALTERNATIVES
Most of this family are too tender to grow outside in Britain. If you do want to try to produce your own passionfruit, you could grow *P. edulis* in a heated greenhouse, as it needs a much warmer temperature range than our weather can provide.

52

A. FRUTESCENS 'JAMAICAN PRIMROSE'

NOT EVERY SUMMER PLANT CAN SIT HAPPILY IN THE GROUND ALL YEAR ROUND AND THERE ARE SOME PLANTS WHICH RICHLY DESERVE A PLACE IN YOUR GARDEN BUT WILL REQUIRE A LITTLE EXTRA ATTENTION.

Half-hardy perennials such as *Argyranthemum frutescens* 'Jamaican Primrose' will bring a light, airy touch to patio displays and sunny borders, but will only survive all year round if you are lucky enough to live in the far south-west of Britain, where the odd cold night will do them no real harm. If there is any likelihood of persistent frost these plants are best treated as annuals and taken out before winter bites or brought into a frost-free place to overwinter.

This is true of many of the plants bought each year for containers and hanging baskets. If you have a place to overwinter them and can learn some basic propagation techniques, plants such as geraniums, tender fuchsias, osteospermums and diascias can be kept from year to year, saving money and bringing a sense of continuity to your displays.

Argyranthemums, often known as Marguerite daisies, in common with many of the other daisy-

type summer flowers, are happiest in full sun and dryish, well-drained conditions. Pinching out the growing tips early on will produce lovely rounded bushy plants.

ALTERNATIVES

For something a little special *Cosmos atrosanguineus*, or the chocolate cosmos, is guaranteed to turn heads and noses to its direction. Not only is it a velvety shade of rich brown but it also has a chocolate scent. What could be better? Or play safe with osteospermums: African daisies that have been bred in a wide range of colours, which will spread merrily at the front of your border throughout the summer months, turning their happy faces to the light of the sun. *Osteospermum* 'Nairobi Purple' is an especially good performer.

53 ANTIRRHINUM MAJUS 'ROYAL BRIDE'

FOR THOSE WHO ARE NOT KEEN ON COMPLICATED AND BRIGHT BEDDING SCHEMES THERE ARE STILL PLENTY OF EASY-TO-GROW ANNUAL PLANTS OF GREAT BEAUTY THAT CAN FILL IN UNEXPECTED GAPS IN THE BORDER.

Antirrhinum majus 'Royal Bride' is an outstanding example of a stylish annual that will fit perfectly in borders and beds, looking as if it truly belongs there. It is an exceptional snapdragon with pure white flowers that stand proud and vertical above its emerald green foliage and the added advantage of fragrance gives it a real edge. It is easily grown from seed sown in a warmish place from March to May.

Regular deadheading will keep it flowering all summer long as will feeding with comfrey or tomato food but, like most annuals, it does not require too rich a programme of feeding as this promotes leaf rather than flower growth. Sun and dry, well-drained conditions will suit it perfectly.

If you do grow snapdragons you may be fortunate to see one of the most delightful sights in any garden: that of a bumble bee wriggling down and disappearing into a snapdragon's throat to get at the nectar inside.

ALTERNATIVES

If seed sowing and planting out seems like too much trouble there are annuals that can be scattered directly into your garden to bring a casual informality and the odd surprising combination to your scheme. The annual poppies, such as *Papaver somniferum* or *Escholzia californica* will pop up wherever they fall, in the shallowest of soils, without you doing anything more than drop them.

Putting it all together

Large border 6 m x 2 m

❶ Syringa vulgaris 'Katherine Havermeyer'

❷ Ceanothus x delineanus 'Gloire de Versailles'

❸ Rosa 'Darcy Bussell'

❹ Lavendula 'Hidcote'

❺ Clematis 'Jackmannii'

❻ Verbena bonariensis

❼ Nepeta 'Six Hills Giant'

❽ Paeonia 'Bowl of Beauty'

❾ Dephinium elatum

❿ Phlox paniculata 'Bright Eyes'

⓫ Allium 'Globemaster'

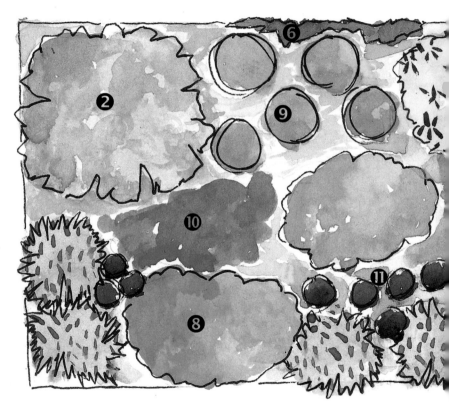

A fabulous, cottage-style summer bed or border using some of our most familiar and best loved plants, this design will provide you with blowsy and romantic blooms, a classic yet relaxed look and plenty of delicious fragrance. Most of these plants will perform better in full sun.

● Place *Ceanothus* x *delineanus* 'Gloire de Versailles' at the back left of your planting area and *Syringa vulgaris* 'Katherine Havermeyer' on the opposite side, giving the *Syringa* a little more space. *Rosa* 'Darcey Bussell' should be planted in the middle towards the front where its fine

THERE IS NOTHING MORE GLORIOUS THAN A SUMMER GARDEN IN
FULL BLOOM — THE COLOURFUL FLOWERS AND SWEET FRAGRANCES
MAKE GARDENING A TRUE PLEASURE.

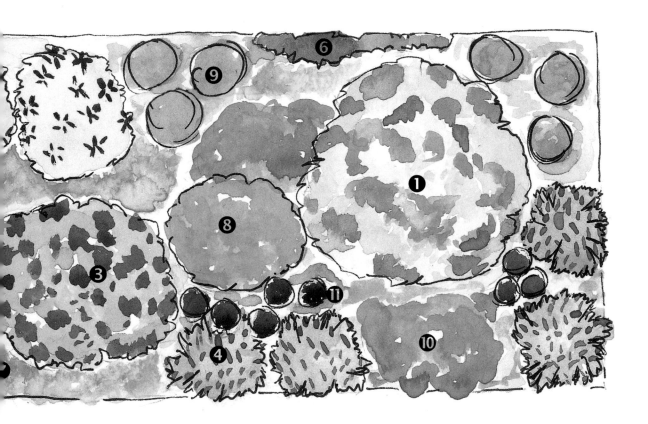

blooms can be fully appreciated.

● Behind *R.* 'Darcey Bussell'
train *Clematis* 'Jackmanii' up a
wigwam of canes or a decorative
support.

● Along the front and sides, plant
Lavendula 'Hidcote' at regular

intervals to bring structure and
unity to the scheme and to provide
a counterpoint to the softness of
the herbaceous planting. Place the
tall, towering spires of *Delphinium
elatum* in groups along the back.

● Fill the middle of the border
with *Phlox paniculata* 'Bright

Eyes' and *Paeonia* 'Bowl of
Beauty' for flowers all summer
long and fill any remaining gaps
with *Nepeta* 'Six Hills Giant'
and natural drifts of *Allium*
'Globemaster' at the front and
Verbena bonariensis towards
the rear.

Easy-care summer side border 5 m x 1 m

In this simple scheme *Fuchsia* 'Mrs Popple', with its hanging red and purple ballet dancer flowers, arch over clumps of *Geranium* 'Johnson's Blue' and a ribbon of pure white *Antirrhinum* 'Royal Bride' for contrast, neither of which will mind being slightly overshadowed. Some sun during the day will be appreciated, though.

❶ Geranium 'Johnson's Blue'
❷ Fuschia 'Mrs Popple'
❸ Antirrhinum 'Royal Bride'

● Plant *Fuchsia* 'Mrs Popple' at the back, underplanted with *Geranium* 'Johnson's Blue.' Plant a thin wavy ribbon of *Antirrhinum* 'Royal Bride' at the front, rather than a straight line.

Small summer semi-circular bed approx 2 m diameter

Whether or not you live near the sea, this design has a distinctly coastal flavour with *Hebe* 'Great Orme' and its pink and white flowers taking centre stage. Take cuttings of *Agyranthemum* 'Jamaica Primrose' if you live in an area prone to frost in winter as it is unlikely to survive all year round outside milder, maritime climates.

❶ Hebe 'Great Orme'
❷ Eryngium alpinum
❸ Agyranthemum 'Jamaican Primrose'

● Plant *Hebe* 'Great Orme' centre back followed by a ribbon of *Eryingium alpinum* and a semicircle of *Agyranthemum* 'Jamaican Primrose' bordering the front for good colour contrast.

SEED SOWING

Most people's first garden experience probably involved planting seeds of some sort or another. Whether it was an early science experiment growing a bean in a jam jar or carefully placing a sunflower seed in the ground, it is almost a rite of passage to adulthood, and nothing beats the pleasure of watching a plant you have sown yourself grow and mature.

Seed sowing is much cheaper than buying plants, and very useful if you have gaps to fill or a larger area to cover quickly. It will also allow you to ring the changes in your garden by introducing quick-flowering annuals or more challenging plants that can't be easily obtained in any other way.

The majority of seed sowing takes place in early spring but autumn sown seeds are also useful, as

they will give you a much earlier flowering the following year. If you only want a few plants sowing in a pot is ideal. Fill a container with seed sowing compost, breaking up any lumps first then sow your seeds lightly before covering with a thin compost layer. Water very gently and make sure they do not dry out as they are germinating. The tricky question of how deep to place a seed is easily solved by a simple rule of thumb: the depth they should be planted should be roughly twice their diameter.

For tender plants, such as the bedding plants for your summer pots, warmth is required so they should be kept on a sunny windowsill or in a heated greenhouse until they have germinated. Hardier plants can usually be left in a cold frame or even outside.

As the soil temperature warms up many seeds can be sown directly into the ground, either in a special seedbed, or directly where they will flower. Sow small amounts in rows to make it easier to identify them and weed around them. First rake the soil to a fine crumb, breaking up lumps with the back of the rake and removing any weeds and large stones. Then use a hoe or trowel to create a v-shaped drill, and sprinkle the seeds along as evenly as possible before gently replacing the soil. Flatten down the drill with the back of a rake. Water well and keep seedlings watered and protected from pests until they are large enough to transplant or can fend for themselves.

For seeds that resent being moved, such as poppies, or for a more natural drift or a larger area, broadcast sowing is a better option. Again this requires some preparation. Weed first and rake the soil to a crumb, breaking up any large clods with the back of the rake or your feet. Only fertilise if you really need to. For a more natural effect mark out the area to sow with sand, keeping the shapes wavy. Then choose

a fine day with no wind (or your seeds will simply blow away). For small seeds add a handful of sand for every metre you plan to sow. This helps with even spreading and allows you to see where you have sown. Divide mix in two then gently sprinkle half back and forth in one direction before turning 45 degrees and doing the same. Once all the seed is sown, rake just enough for the seeds to settle into the ground but not enough to push them around. Water gently and protect with netting if birds are a real problem.

Opposite left Traditionally, terracotta pots would have been used but these days plastic is more useful.

Opposite right Seed sowing in some cases literally involves just sprinkling a packet of seeds over compost.

Above A colourful display of poppies produced from just a small packet of seeds.

SUMMER POTS AND PATIO DISPLAYS

It is easy enough to put a plant or two in a pot but creating a fabulous summer display that will impress everyone takes a little more thought. There is such a plethora of plants to choose from that garden style often goes out of the window in favour of cramming as many blooms as possible in as many pots as you can get hold of. Instant colour and gratification can easily have a messy result. If you wouldn't countenance brash colours and random planting in your beds and borders then you shouldn't countenance this on your patio either.

It is far better to pick a style and theme for your summer pots and stick to it. A row of red geraniums in similar classic terracotta pots looks wonderfully stylish, or try pots of different sizes grouped together containing a wider range of plants in similar tones. Whatever you choose the size of the pot should be suitable for your plant choice.

If you do want mixed planting in your pots stick to three or five different varieties of plant. One taller for the middle or back to add height, one or two medium-sized plant varieties to fill in the centre and one or two varieties around the edge, preferably trailing over. Before you plant you should group the plants in the pot and see how they look before actually planting them in.

As a rule of thumb good-looking pots require three things: the right compost, the right drainage and the right watering regime. Always make sure that the container you plan to use has drainage holes then fill the bottom with a layer of gravel or broken pots to ensure your plants will never sit in waterlogged soil. All-purpose compost is fine for many plants but check first to see if your plant choice does require specialist compost. Adding water-retaining granules and slow-release food will also help your pots to look good for longer, although many modern composts already contain such additives. Remember, too, that pots need more water than the garden in general, so must be checked regularly, in most cases on a daily

Left Seedlings in the greenhouse at Cotehele, Cornwall.

Opposite above Growing in containers is also useful if you think you might move house.

Opposite left An assortment of different size pots can make an attractive planting composition.

Opposite below right For the price of a few bulbs you can have a riot of colour in your containers.

AUTUMN

THE SUN IS LOWER in the sky in autumn. Rather than bright, glaring light from above, a softer, subdued colour appears to shine through the plants, giving them a translucent, almost effervescent quality. Different shadows and shapes are created among the plants making us see them in a whole different light and showing off what would otherwise be unnoticed qualities in their texture and form. While some plants start to retreat back into the soil, many others refuse to go forth into the cold months without a spectacular flurry of colour and a final fling of exuberance. Leaves on many of the trees, such as acer, sorbus and stewartia take on the hot, fiery colours, while birch and beech supply the soft, mellow, buttery tones as a warming backdrop. There is also an understorey of a rich supply of colourful berries and fruit bursting out of the garden with unfettered passion, including elderberries, grapevines and malus trees coming in a range of hues.

Closer to the ground there are still lots of late flowering herbaceous plants, such as heleniums, asters, chrysanthemums, sedums and dahlias lighting up the darker evenings putting a smile on the faces of the gardeners. Even the naked ladies, the colchicums, come out to put on a show, with just their pinkish purple flowers being revealed.

Despite the freshness in the air, there is a romantic cosiness about autumn, as the oppressive heat of summer softens to a more pleasant temperature. It feels as if a new phase in the gardener's calendar has begun. It's a time for folklore, harvest festivals, homemade jam, cider and wine, and for celebrating the season past and the future fun that will be had in the garden. It's a season when bonfires are lit outside in the evenings and the smell of wood-smoke pervades the garden. It's a period of earthy odours too, when the moisture rises in the air and gardeners start to look towards the engine house of the garden, the compost heap.

Previous page A red acer in the Arboretum in autumn at Bodnant Garden, Conwy.

Left Herbaceous border in autumn at Bodnant Garden, Conwy.

54 Sorbus aucuparia, Rowan Tree

A NATIVE TREE OF EUROPE THAT GROWS WILDLY IN THE NATURAL
LANDSCAPE, YET IS RESTRAINED AND CULTURED ENOUGH TO BE A
STAR PERFORMER IN THE GARDEN, THE ROWAN TREE PROVIDES A
SPECTACULAR SHOW WITH ITS AUTUMN COLOUR AND BRIGHT BERRIES.

There are many ornamental sorbus available to buy for the garden but *Sorbus aucuparia* is by far the most popular. It forms an upright deciduous tree with a neat, rounded habit growing to an eventual height of about 10m (33ft) making it a suitable for small- to medium-sized gardens. It forms masses of sweet scented (almost sickly) clusters of white flowers in spring. But its real moment of glory is autumn, for two reasons: firstly, the bright orange and red berries that hang off the branches in large bunches are produced in abundance; and secondly, the foliage that appears in similar fiery colours to complement the fruit. The fruit can be used in cooking with rowan jelly being a popular accompaniment to game dishes. It is packed full of vitamin C and in the past has been used as a treatment for scurvy. However, you'll be lucky if you can get to the berries before the birds, which absolutely love this tree making it a good choice if you want to attract wildlife into your garden.

Its position in the garden can be very flexible. In nature it is often found growing in woodlands as an understorey tree under taller ones in the secondary canopy, making it well-suited to shady conditions in the garden too. However, they can also appear as solitary trees on the tops of hills, on chalky downland or, as its other common name suggests – mountain ash – on the sides of mountains. It is therefore perfectly suitable for growing as a single, solitary specimen in the open too, and makes a wonderful individual specimen on a lawn, particularly when underplanted with autumnal bulbs such as colchicums or autumn crocus. It is a tough tree this one, very hardy, and there isn't much that will fell it. It has been found in the UK growing up to heights of 1,000m (3,300ft) on mountainsides albeit as a much more restricted size, more like a shrub.

Don't be deceived though by the common name 'ash'. They're not related so won't suffer from any of the 'ash dieback' issues. The common name association is because they have similar leaflet patterns in opposite pairs along the stems.

ALTERNATIVES

In really small gardens an ideal choice is the variety 'Fastigiata', which forms a narrow and slow growing tree. 'Crème Lace' has a delicate habit, which forms creamy white berries, while 'Dirkenii' is a slightly unusual golden-leaved form with an upright habit and produces lots of red berries.

55

ACER PALMATUM 'BLOODGOOD'

WITH ITS ATTRACTIVE, DEEPLY LOBED LEAVES THAT TURN AN AMAZING VIVID RED IN AUTUMN, THIS JAPANESE MAPLE MAKES A WONDERFUL SPECIMEN TREE IN A SMALL TO MEDIUM-SIZED GARDEN OR FOR GROWING IN A LARGE CONTAINER.

There are many Japanese acers available, ranging from a mere 1m high to trees that reach as high as a two-storey house. With their attractive cut-shaped leaves and their wonderful, brightly coloured autumnal foliage, Japanese maples are one of the quintessential trees for a small garden.

'Bloodgood' is one of the more modestly sized trees, reaching to between 2.5m and 4m high after about 10 years. They are naturally woodland plants, preferring to grow in dappled shade, but will tolerate a modest amount of sun.

Although the trees themselves are very hardy, the new growth can be susceptible to harsh cold weather so it is best to avoid frost pockets. As with most acers, they also require shelter from strong winds, which can quickly decimate their foliage. Their ideal soil is slightly acidic although there are other acers that will tolerate moderate amounts of chalk. Avoid water-logged soil or extremely dry conditions. Acers have a shallow fibrous root system, so adding organic matter such as leaf mould should ensure there is enough moist but free-draining soil just below the surface of the ground. Mulching around the base of

the tree each year with more compost will help to retain moisture and suppress weeds that compete for nutrients.

They are slow-growing trees, making them easy to maintain. Little pruning is required of them, as they produce their best shape when allowed to naturally grow without removing many branches. However, it may occasionally be necessary to do some remedial pruning if branches are rubbing on each other. The best time to do this is from late autumn to late winter.

ALTERNATIVES

Other acers worth trying include *Acer palmatum* 'Sango kaku', which has amazing red branches and trunk making it a wonderful feature all year round. It also produces attractive green leaves that turn a stunning golden yellow in autumn. *Acer palmatum* 'Osakazuki' forms a spectacular display of hot scarlet-coloured foliage prior to their leaves dropping off.

56 STEWARTIA PSEUDOCAMELLIA

A SMALL- TO MEDIUM-SIZED TREE THAT REALLY DOES HAVE IT ALL!
ATTRACTIVE, PEELING WINTER BARK, GREAT AUTUMN COLOUR AND
A SPRING COVERING OF SHOWY WHITE FLOWERS, THE JAPANESE
STEWARTIA REALLY EARNS ITS KEEP IN THE GARDEN.

The most alluring aspect for me about this tree from Japan and Korea is the peeling bark, better than any ornamental birch or cherry tree. The trunk starts to peel from a young age in rich warm colours, such as cinnamon, copper, and red. It also has one of the best autumnal foliage displays of all the ornamental trees, making it amazing value for money.

Stewartia pseudocamellia or false camellia is so called because in summer it is covered with blooms with cup-shaped white flowers with a rich, orangey yellow centre. It is in fact closely related to the camellia, coming from the same family *Theaceae*, and is often referred to as 'deciduous camellia'.

This tree is slow growing, but after five to ten years it will start to earn its keep as a star performer all year round. Most people prefer to grow it as a multi-stemmed tree to maximise the 'peeling bark' appeal, but it can equally be grown as a single trunk. To grow it as a multi-stemmed tree it may need pruning back to about knee height when young to encourage new stems, although quite often it will naturally send out young shoots.

They require slightly acidic, moist but free-draining soil and prefer dappled shade. Mulch regularly around the base of the tree in its formative years to suppress any weeds and retain the moisture. Do take time in selecting the final planting place for the tree as they don't respond well or quickly to being transplanted due to their slow growing nature.

ALTERNATIVES
S. monadelpha, otherwise known as the 'tall stewartia' (apparently it grows up to 20m/65ft in the wild), has gorgeous, smooth, cinnamon brown bark, and is much smaller when grown under cultivation in a garden.

57

SAMBUCUS NIGRA 'GERDA'

MOST PEOPLE ARE FAMILIAR WITH THE COMMON ELDER TREE BUT THIS DARK-LEAVED VARIETY IS SOMETHING A BIT SPECIAL, MAKING A SUPERB FEATURE IN THE GARDEN AS EITHER A SPECIMEN PLANT OR AT THE BACK OF THE BORDER.

Its alternative name 'Black Beauty' describes this deciduous shrub perfectly. The dark foliage and berries makes it a really head-turning stunner in the garden. The clusters of flat-headed flowers appear in early summer and have a fresh, almost citrusy scent to them. The berries appear from late summer onwards and are glossy and shiny black, and can be used to make elderberry cordial, elderberry jelly or, my favourite, elderberry wine. However, do be warned, the birds love this plant and will quickly strip the berries at the first signs of them ripening, so it may be worth draping a net over them if you want to use them yourself.

It forms a very small tree or large shrub about 3–4m (10–13ft) high and the same in its spread, so is ideal for planting towards the back of a deep border. If you want to grow the tree purely for its foliage effect then it can be cut back hard, almost to ground level, to encourage lots of luxuriant new stems, but this will be at the sacrifice of the flowers and fruit. Alternatively grow it as a small specimen tree or shrub, or even in a pot, where it will make an eye-catching feature or focal point. It will just occasionally require the removal of crossing or dying branches in winter. A containerised plant can be planted at any time of the year, but the best time to get it established is early autumn when the soil is still warm. Keep the plant well-watered in its first season after planting. It will also benefit from a layer of mulch at the base of its trunk in early spring.

It grows equally well in full sun or dappled shade. It's dead easy to propagate too as it readily produces suckers out of the ground, which can be dug up with a section of root attached and stuck into a pot of compost to grow on for a few weeks before planting out.

ALTERNATIVES
The two other common ornamental sambucus that can be found easily in garden centres are 'Black Lace', which is similar to 'Black Beauty' except it has the most exquisite, finely cut leaves. It's well worth purchasing if you come across it. The other popular one is *S. nigra* 'Aurea', which has spectacular golden foliage.

58 COTINUS 'GRACE'

AS THE SUN'S STRENGTH STARTS TO WANE WITH THE ARRIVAL OF
AUTUMN, THE INCREASINGLY MELLOW LIGHT PICKS UP THE TONAL
HUES OF THE SMOKE BUSH LEAVES AND MAKES THIS SHRUB GLEAM
WITH COPPER RICHNESS.

Cotinus coggyria is a shrub loved by landscape
designers for its head-turning good looks and is often
seen planted as a specimen. This is a shame as it is
one of those plants that interacts with other colors
in the garden and brings out the best in everything
planted close by. It is much more interesting in the
back of the mixed border than standing alone.

Cotinus are very unfussy about conditions as long as
they are in as much sun as possible. They are hardy,
deciduous and vigorous, reaching over 5m (16½ft)
tall, with simple, rounded leaves and can easily be
pruned as a tree to fit smaller spaces. In the case of
these plants it is all about the colour.

C. 'Grace' is especially lovely, with leaves of reddish
brown tinged with purple, the colour of a well-
burnished copper pot, throughout the summer
months. Given light and warmth it will also flower
at this time. Clouds of insubstantial plumes of tiny
flowers billow out in every direction, hence the name
smoke bush, but for the highlight of the show you
have to wait until autumn. As the days shorten, the
colours of *C. 'Grace'* intensify; the reds get richer, the
purple becomes pinker, the undersides become more
orange and the whole shrub begins to glow and blaze
in the sun. When the herbaceous plants nearby begin
their decline, the colours of *C. 'Grace'* soften and
complement the fading scene. Straw-like grasses and
seedheads, the brown stems of herbaceous plants, the
gently faded colours of late flowers – all become part
of a rich, autumnal oil painting.

ALTERNATIVES
C. 'Grace' is not the only choice as a backdrop
to hot red and yellow planting schemes. The
vivid burgundy-purple tones of *C. coggyria*
'Royal Purple' will also work well. The
darker purple of this plant will also liven up
whites, lemons and pale apricots.

59 CORNUS KOUSA VAR. CHINENSIS

A SHRUB OR SMALL TREE FOR ALL SEASONS, THIS SPREADING CORNUS FROM CHINA PROVIDES CREAMY WHITE FLOWER BRACTS DURING SPRING, LARGE, STRAWBERRY-LIKE FRUITS LATER IN THE SEASON AND SHOWSTOPPING FOLIAGE COLOURS IN AUTUMN.

You get good value for money with this small, spreading tree that has so much to offer. The fruit is very impressive in autumn with what look like massive, deep red strawberry fruits covering the tree. The fruit is edible and is often made into jam and alcoholic beverages in Japan and China.

In most places it is deciduous, with the foliage turning magnificent colours of orange, red and purple, but in milder climates it retains its foliage during winter. In early summer this broad, billowing tree is covered with large, showy creamy white bracts, often mistakenly identified as the flowers, but actually the insignificant centres to the bracts. Another rewarding aspect of this tree is the foliage, which forms interesting mottled patterns and is shown off to its best effect in winter when the spreading branches are denuded of their foliage.

The tree doesn't get too big in the garden, usually reaching about 4–5m (13–16½ft) high and in spread. It is quite happy in partial shade or full sun and because of its reasonably compact nature is suitable for most small to medium gardens. They will tolerate most soils and will often withstand waterlogging although their favoured soil is moist but well drained. It is best planted at the back of a deep border or as a specimen tree where its constant changes in the season can be regularly admired.

The tree is pretty much maintenance free. It may occasionally need remedial pruning purely to retain its shape, although pruning is generally not encouraged. Mulching around the tree with rotted organic matter is recommended.

ALTERNATIVES
C. kousa 'Miss Satomi' is an elegant shrub from Japan with great autumn foliage and deep pink bracts in early summer. The variety 'Snow Boy' is an interesting variety of *kousa* because of its variegated foliage in shades of grey and green with a white margin.

HYDRANGEAS ARE ONE OF THE CLASSIC EARLY AUTUMN SHRUBS, PRODUCING LARGE FLOWERING HEADS THAT RANGE FROM DEEP REDS TO BRIGHT BLUES. 'MARIESII PERFECTA' IS A POPULAR LACECAP VARIETY, PRODUCING LARGE, BLUE OR PINK FLOWERHEADS.

Also known as 'Blue Wave', I grow this plant on a steep bank at the National Trust's Greenway gardens in Devon and the effect is mesmerising, with the large blue lacecaps looking as though they are a cascading waterfall. There are loads of macrophylla types of hydrangea, divided up into two distinct categories: mopheads, which produce large domed flowerheads that make impressive dried cut flower displays, and lacecaps, which produce a flatter flower with tiny, almost glossy clusters of flowers in the centre, surrounded by almost papery-like petals.

'Blue Wave' is one of the latter categories and the tiny flowers in the centre look like miniature nuggets of the bluest sapphires. Hydrangeas can be grown in soil with a wide range of pH levels and this affects the colour of the flower, with them ranging between red and blue, with acidic conditions making them more blue. The flowers of 'Blue Wave' turn a mauve-pink colour in alkaline conditions.

In the garden they're a useful shrub for providing masses of flowers in late summer and early autumn when most other woody plants have finished.

They are tolerant of shade and are a popular choice for woodland gardens where they work well as a shrub canopy under larger trees. They are equally suited to being grown in full sun and are ideal for planting in a shrub border or as a backdrop to an herbaceous flower bed. They also look great in traditional cottage garden designs and make a good, sturdy, upright structure when grown among sprawling herbaceous plants, rambling roses and loose drifts of annuals. My favourite place to see them though is *en masse* or lining a path or edge of a garden.

Hydrangeas are reasonably hardy, but in cooler areas it is worth holding back on the pruning until mid-spring as the flowerheads offer the plant some frost and winter protection. They flower on wood produced the previous year, and should be pruned by cutting back the old flowering stems by about a third to a pair of healthy buds.

ALTERNATIVES

There are lots of mophead and lacecap types of hydrangeas to choose from, but some of the species are interesting too. *Hydrangea petiolaris* is the climbing hydrangea, which is self-clinging and can be trained up a wall or even into a tree, covering the area with creamy white lacecap-type flowers that can be as large as 25cm (10in) across. *H. paniculata* is another popular species of hydrangea that produces huge, long panicles of flowers on new growth. For maximum flower size the new stems formed the previous year should be pruned back to a couple of buds in early spring. They are ideal plants for lining a woodland path or to create a small avenue. One of the most popular varieties of *paniculata* is 'Grandiflora' with large clusters of creamy white flowers.

61 SEDUM SPECTABILE 'RUBY GLOW'

FROM LATE SUMMER TO LATE AUTUMN THIS HERBACEOUS PERENNIAL APPEARS TO RADIATE WITH ITS SUMPTUOUS RUBY-RED FLOWERHEADS HELD ALOFT ABOVE ITS FLESHY LEAVES. THE EFFECT IS MESMERISING AND ONE OF THE HIGHLIGHTS OF THE AUTUMNAL BORDER.

Sedum spectabile 'Ruby Glow' is a mound-forming perennial succulent, grown for its fleshy leaves and deeply coloured flowerheads that appears towards the end of summer. The flowers are starry-shaped and crimson, held aloft on dark red stems about 30cm (12in) off the ground to mesmerising effect. It requires full sun and free-draining soil and is well-suited to dry or gravel gardens. The green, fleshy leaves have an attractive purplish tinge to them, providing interest for most of the year. Prior to the flowers opening, 'Ruby Glow' has masses of tiny, pointed, dark pink buds.

In really mild winters or sheltered conditions the star-shaped flowers can persist into the New Year. The deep, velvety colour of this variety has an almost Michaelmas feel to it that reminds me of the colour of a traditional Father Christmas' suit, or a glass of mulled wine. Either way the rich, warm tones look like you could almost warm your hands and cook marshmallows on the plant. The glowing colour combines nicely with evergreens like holly or conifers such as low growing junipers. Closer to the ground and earlier in autumn, it's lovely to see its rich, fleshy foliage contrasted with warm coloured grasses such as *Anemanthele lessoniana*, New Zealand wind grass (formley *Stipa arundinaacea*), *Calamagrostis brachytricha* or *Miscanthus sinensis* 'Kleine Silberspinne'.

The best thing about this plant is when the low autumnal sun catches the succulent foliage and ruby-red flowers, giving it an almost translucent look. Bees, hoverflies and butterflies love sedum as it is a great source of food for them as flowering plants become scarcer when temperatures take a dip.

Sedums generally require little care. Sometimes the flowers can be so large that they become top heavy and snap their stems. This particularly happens in wet autumns when the flowers hold onto moisture and become too heavy to support. To avoid this it may be necessary to stake them. After flowering, the heads can be cut back to tidy them up and maintain their shape. Plants can be divided after flowering in winter if it is mild, or in early spring.

ALTERNATIVES

There are lots of sedums suitable for the border available, the most popular being *S. spectabile* 'Autumn Joy' with flowers that start off pale pink and develop to a rusty red colour as they mature. Another interesting one to try is 'Mr Goodbud', which is a more compact, dwarf form. It reaches up to 60cm (2ft) tall and has large, grey-green leaves tinged purple, and clusters of pale pink flowers. I particularly love *S. telephium* 'Purple Emperor', which produces wide panicles of ruby-red flowers and has wonderful burgundy-black flesh foliage. Ideal for the front of a border and best planted *en masse* for the most dramatic effect. The other popular type of sedums that are used are the much smaller and compact types used on green roofs and in rockeries. Popular choices include *S. album*, *S. acre* and *S. oreganum*.

Helenium
'Moerheim Beauty'

THE COLOURS OF THIS PERENNIAL HELENIUM EPITOMISE THE RICH HAZY TONES YOU EXPECT IN AN EARLY WARM AUTUMNAL FLOWER BORDER WITH ITS SULTRY REDDISH ORANGE, DAISY-SHAPED FLOWERS HELD ALOFT ON THEIR WIRY STEMS.

Heleniums are one of the classic daisy-shaped herbaceous perennials that are currently so much in fashion alongside asters, rudbeckias and echinaccas, and seen so much in prairie-style gardens. They are prolific flowerers providing a good solid backbone in the border during late summer and autumn.

They originate from North America and their petals come in rich hues of red, orange and copper with the round centre of the flower looking like a rich chocolate button. It is commonly known as sneezeweed because Cherokee Native Americans used to dry the flowers as a cure for the common cold. They are generally drought resistant and easy to maintain. They also make great cut flowers, and butterflies and bees seem to love them.

There are lots of heleniums to choose from but *Helenium* 'Moerheim Beauty' is one of the most popular. This stunning herbaceous perennial reaches up to 1.2m (4ft) high, so should be placed in the middle or towards the back of the border. Plant

them in clusters of three, five or seven depending on the size of the bed at about 45cm (18in) apart. Add plenty of organic matter to the soil prior to planting. They may well need supporting with hazel sticks to prevent their flowerheads from flopping over. The plants can be left to turn to seed as they can still look dramatic in winter, but should be cut back in early spring.

They'll benefit from being divided every couple of years after they have finished flowering, either in winter if it is mild enough, or early spring.

They are real sun lovers and prefer well-drained conditions to perform at their best. They combine with other, really hot, sizzling plants, such as kniphofia (red hot pokers) and rubeckias. They also look great with ornamental grasses if you want to try and get that loose 'prairie' style of planting in your garden.

ALTERNATIVES

There are literally hundreds to choose from, but some of the most popular are: *H.* 'Ruby Tuesday', a compact variety reaching about 50cm (20in) in height with plenty of small, dark red flowers; 'Sahin's Early Flowerer' has orange flowerheads and is a great choice if you want to inject a bit of colour earlier on into the border as it flowers a good few weeks before the others; for a yellow variety 'Butter Pat' is a good reliable choice, producing a profusion of flowers from late summer onwards.

63 EUONYMUS ALATUS 'COMPACTUS'

THIS IS AN EXTREMELY EYE-CATCHING AND POPULAR SHRUB WITH SHOWY AUTUMNAL FOLIAGE THAT TURNS BRIGHT RED AS SUMMER STARTS TO FADE.

Often called 'winged spindle' because of the distinctive corky wings on its branches, this slow growing shrub is a real curiosity in the garden. The leaves are dark green during the summer when it also flowers, producing pale yellow, fairly insignificant flowers.

It's real showpiece is in autumn where it lives up to its other common name of 'burning bush', putting on a spectacular foliage display with shades of crimson, oranges, reds and scarlet. 'Compactus' is ideal for a small garden, reaching only about 1m (3ft) in height and spread, and is ideal for growing in a container or on a patio or balcony. It can be used to create a low, dense hedge.

If you want something bigger then the plain *Euonymous alatus* is a better choice, being a medium-sized, densely branching shrub reaching about 1–2.5m (3–8ft) in height and a 3m (10ft) spread with more pronounced corky 'wings'.

They both prefer full sun or partial shade and are tolerant of most soil regardless of whether it is sand or clay, but it needs to be fertile.

Maintenance is easy, simply pruning out damaged or crossed branches in late winter to spring. Wayward branches can also be cut back at this time to improve its shape. The shrub also benefits from a mulch in early spring with well-rotted manure or garden compost.

ALTERNATIVES
If you want even more impressive autumnal fruit try *E. phellomanus* or *E. planipes*. Another popular type of euonymus are the *fortunei* species, which have a low spreading habit and occasionally used to trail over low walls or as a ground cover plant. 'Emerald 'n' Gold' is one of the popular types.

64 RUDBECKIA FULGIDA 'GOLDSTURM'

RUDBECKIAS ARE CLASSIC PLANTS OF THE PRAIRIE STYLE, ASSOCIATING BRILLIANTLY WITH ORNAMENTAL GRASSES AND CREATING GREAT, FLAT DRIFTS OF UNASHAMED BOLDNESS THAT YOU JUST HAVE TO ADMIRE.

The most complicated thing about the rudbeckia is its name. The bright, bold, golden daisy blooms of the coneflower are not subtle or nuanced but they make a dramatic statement at the end of summer and are easy plants to look after, requiring very little in the way of intervention. They even do well in heavy soils, although they will still appreciate any efforts to improve the conditions. Mostly though, sun, moderate access to moisture and the occasional dividing up of clumps if they get too congested is all they will require to flourish from August right through to October.

Rudbeckia fulgida var. *sullivantii* 'Goldsturm' is an excellent example of this plant. The flowers are around 12cm (4½in) across, a deep golden colour, more like the eggs of corn-fed chickens than the insipid yellow of battery eggs, and usually grow to around 80cm (2½ft), roughly knee height. The brown cones in the centre stand quite proud above the petals and are particularly noticeable as each flowerhead points upwards directly towards the open sky.

ALTERNATIVES

For really dramatic impact at the back of the border, *R. laciniata* 'Herbstsonne' will grow up to 2.5m (8ft) tall. You might also enjoy the curious flower of *R. occidentalis* 'Green Wizard', the petals of which are thin and green and are only a sideshow to the bulbous centre cone. A sculptural oddity.

65

ECHINACEA PURPUREA

BRINGING JOY TO EVERYONE, ECHINACEA PURPUREA MAY BE SHORT
LIVED BUT ITS ROSY MAUVE FLOWERS AND HEDGEHOG APPEARANCE
ARE WONDERFUL ADDITIONS TO ANY WILDLIFE-FRIENDLY GARDEN,
WHERE IT WILL ATTRACT BEES, BUTTERFLIES AND LATER BIRDS.

Echinaceas, like their cousins, the rudbeckias, are
native to the great prairies of the United States.
They are perhaps best known as an herbal remedy
for colds but their medical qualities are only part
of the story. These are orange-centred coneflowers,
a colour that seems to work perfectly with the
petals to create tonal harmony, which make a great
statement drifting through a border.

At around 1.2m (4ft) tall they are better off towards
the back of a planting scheme, although their flower
stems are pretty sturdy so neither shelter nor staking
should be required.

Like all daisy types they are natural sun lovers and
will steadfastly refuse to flower if planted anywhere
at all shady. They also dislike being in soggy ground
and this may be why they do not always survive
over winter. It is not a lack of hardiness but their
preference for a cold, dry winter rather than a
mild, wet one that is the cause of any sudden loss.
This makes them, however, a good choice for dry,
sandy soil.

They flower earlier than rudbeckias and asters, but
even if they have lost their petals in the autumn
as the others are proudly continuing to flower, the
cones, full of seed, still provide plenty of interest
and a ready food source for numerous birds.

ALTERNATIVES
A few variations of this plant are available
if you wish to try something different. *E.
purpurea* 'Ruby Glow' has bigger flowers.
Or, for a change, try *E. purpurea* 'Alba',
an elegant combination of white and
pale green.

66

ASTER X FRIKARTII 'MONCH'

THE STARRY FLOWERS OF THE ASTER ARE A GODSEND IN AUTUMN, DRAWING THE EYE AWAY FROM FAST-FADING EARLY PERENNIALS WITH THEIR JOLLY SWEET-SHOP COLOURS AND HAPPY, RELAXED NATURE.

Mention asters and many gardeners will shake their heads and mutter the dreaded words – powdery mildew. Asters, or Michaelmas daisies, are prone to this affliction, it is especially a problem for the asters bred in America whose natural habitat is marshland and which are weakened by the drier conditions of most gardens. *Aster* x *frikartii* has more suitable parentage, though, and so is the least susceptible of all the commonly available asters to mildew attacks and copes better in hot, dry weather.

The leaves of *A.* x *frikartii* 'Monch' are rather rough and ready, but this hardly matters as the plant is delightfully free flowering and the flowers, with their mauve double row of petals with gold centre, are all you will notice. Its slightly lax habit makes it a good choice to plant with ornamental grasses as well as in an herbaceous border, where it will hide the early casualties under its wings. It holds up well enough, however, not to need staking, averaging about 80cm (2½ft) in height.

Aster do best in areas with cool and moist summers, and love cold nights, but they will not complain about being a little warmer and drier as long as the soil is in reasonable condition. A good mulch will help to keep the plants cooler and to conserve water. Your aster should flower from July right the way through to October so it is well worth its place. Butterflies adore it equally, offering them plenty of welcome late nectar as the season shortens.

ALTERNATIVES
A. 'Little Carlow' is also mildew resistant with a more intense violet blue flower while *A. novae angliae* 'Harrington's Pink' is a delightful shade of pretty pink but would probably need regular spraying to prevent an attack.

67

ANENOME X HYBRIDA
'HONORINE JOBERT'

A WONDERFUL HERBACEOUS PLANT FOR BRIGHTENING UP A DARK OR SHADY CORNER, THIS JAPANESE ANEMONE PRODUCES MASSES OF ELEGANT WHITE FLOWERS ON UPRIGHT TALL STEMS FROM LATE SUMMER UNTIL LATE AUTUMN.

This is a much utilised late summer border perennial, and is indispensable for providing backbone to muted colour combinations with its pure white, cup-shaped flowers with yellow stamens. They work well in pastel colour schemes and provide a useful calming alternative to some of the other brighter, autumnal plants, such as red hot pokers and more garish dahlias. *Anemone* x *hybrida* 'Honorine Jobert' is fully hardy and stands tall and proud at over 1.5m (5ft) high, dismissing anything the unreliable, tempestuous, autumnal weather can throw at it. It isn't fussy about its location either, happy in sun or partial shade, but ideally prefers a moist, free-draining and fertile soil.

'Honorine Jobert' is an old variety dating back over 150 years and as its name suggests was discovered in France. Often used in gardens in the shade of trees or to brighten drab corners, the elegant, cup-shaped white flowers also look fantastic contrasted with dark, hard landscaping structures, such as buildings, sheds and walls or evergreen foliage such as a yew or holly hedge. I love to see them planted near the edge of a pond (avoid boggy or wet ground), where their flowers get picked up in the reflections, while their hardy foliage provides shelter for visiting wildlife.

The large, vine-shaped leaves add additional ornamental qualities, and in some of the milder areas of Britain, can be visible most of the year.

It would be a lie to say *A*. x *hybrida* 'Honorine Jobert' is low-maintenance. It can be invasive and prone to spreading through the flower beds. Although this variety isn't as vigorous as *A*. x *hybrida*, it has still inherited its fondness to stray from its intended home. Its invasive tendencies and impulse to explore will have to be kept an eye on if it isn't to encroach onto another plant's patch.

It should be cut back and tidied up in spring. In addition it benefits from a good 5cm (2in) deep mulch of well-rotted manure or compost around the base of the plants to ensure their leaves remain lush and they flower prolifically. If the plant does start to get too big for its space then it can be lifted and divided in early spring.

ALTERNATIVES

A. x *hybrid* is the most popular garden variety with pale pink flowers but it can be invasive. There are a number of other varieties such as 'Königin Charlotte', which has large, rose-pink, semi-double flowers or 'Whirlwind' with semi-double white flowers and 'Andrea Atkinson' with white flowers tinged with pink and green on the outside.

A. huphehensis 'Hadspen Abundance' is a classic later flowering border perennial with reddish pink flowers tinged white at the tips.

68

KNIPHOFIA
'ROYAL STANDARD'

THIS IS ONE OF THE MOST POPULAR AND CLASSIC RED HOT POKERS THAT APPEARS IN MIDSUMMER AND PERSISTS RIGHT THROUGH INTO AUTUMN. ITS BOLD, HOT COLOURS MAKE IT A STRIKING PERFORMER IN THE HERBACEOUS BORDER OR SUB-TROPICAL BEDS.

Originating from South Africa, kniphofia produces large, spiky flowerheads, which are, not surprisingly, a similar shape and colour to the tips of a red hot poker. *Kniphofia* 'Royal Standard' simply sizzles in the border when it makes its much anticipated first appearance in midsummer.

It is one of the older varieties and produces flowers up to 1m (3ft) in height, making them suitable for the middle or back of an herbaceous border. In smaller gardens they can be grown in warm, sunny island beds as clumps of exotic-looking features in their own right.

It also looks great when grown in terracotta or bright ceramic flower pots on the patio. It has bright red buds that develop into colourful golden yellow flowers, but the intriguing aspect I love most about this plant is that the effect is very gradual, with the buds opening from the bottom upwards. This means that for much of the season there is an eye-catching, two-tone effect on the spike, with yellow at the base of the flower and red towards the top. The plant also has strap-like, evergreen foliage that frames the vertical flower stems perfectly.

Kniphofia likes a deep, moist but well-drained soil, so it is worth preparing the soil well before planting by digging it over and adding lots of organic matter, such as well-rotted manure or garden compost. Cut back the spent flower stems in late autumn to tidy the plant up. In spring they can be cut back harder to near ground level to encourage fresher foliage and create more space for the emerging growth.

They are very easy to grow and once planted will literally blaze away. They are often used in sub-tropical planting schemes, despite being very hardy themselves, with their hot colours and striking bold, upright structures making them an ideal and obvious choice. They combine nicely with some of the other warm-coloured, late flowering perennials such as heleniums (sneezeweed) and rudbeckias (black-eyed Susan) as well as some of the richly coloured dahlias, such as 'Bishop of Llandaff' or the strappy foliage and bright red flowers of *Crocosmia* 'Lucifer'. They also look great among a backdrop of ornamental grasses.

ALTERNATIVES

There are hundreds to choose from but one of the most popular is *K.* 'Little Maid', which is more subtle, producing pale buff yellow or ivory flowers in late summer and early autumn. It is much smaller than 'Royal Standard', growing to only about 50cm (20in), making it suitable for the front of a flower border or for growing in containers. *K. rooperi* grows to about 1.2m (4ft) and has impressive rounded and tightly tubular flowers that are bright red but fade to yellow.

69 PENSTEMON 'GARNET'

PRODUCING A GENEROUS MASS OF FLOWER SPIKES, PENSTEMON BRINGS
A LIGHT AND ATTRACTIVE TOUCH TO LATE SUMMER AND AUTUMN
PLANTINGS WHEN THE BIGGER, BOLDER FLOWERS ARE VYING TO CATCH
YOUR EYE.

The major issue to be aware of when considering
penstemons is their hardiness. The possibility always
exists that a really hard winter will do away with
your beloved plants but there are some easy steps
to take to mitigate the effects of a long period of
frost, such as postponing cutting back until spring or
taking cuttings ready for replanting.

Penstemon 'Garnet' appears to be one of, if not the,
hardiest of the penstemons, as well as being a very
beautiful plant. As its name suggests it has deep
red flowers, and is one of the taller penstemons
available so it may need some twiggy sticks to keep
it upright. Alternatively, plant it where surrounding
plants will support it. It is especially good at setting
off the greens of other foliage plants.

Apart from the hardiness factor penstemons are very
easy to grow. They require only average conditions
to flourish, will tolerate heavy and light soils and
simply need cutting back hard once a year to
prevent legginess. Regular deadheading will keep
them flowering for longer.

ALTERNATIVES
P. 'Blackbird' is probably the sultriest of the border penstemons, with
a rich, velvet, dark maroon colour. For a more cottage garden look
try *P.* 'Apple Blossom', pink and white or *P.* 'Heavenly Blue', a muted
shade somewhere between blue and mauve.

70 SCHIZOSTYLIS COCCINEA 'MAJOR'

THIS IS A BRIGHT, CHEERY AND TROUBLE-FREE HERBACEOUS PERENNIAL THAT WILL BRIGHTEN UP THE COLDEST AUTUMN DAY. HAILING FROM SOUTH AFRICA, IT WILL KEEP FLOWERING FOR MOST OF AUTUMN AND SOMETIMES RIGHT UP UNTIL CHRISTMAS IN MILDER WINTERS.

When it comes to generosity, this plant has it in bucketloads. When most of the herbaceous perennials are shrinking back into the soil at the mere thought of cooler and wetter weather, schizostylis rears its flowering head and starts to do its thing! It thrives in most soils, but prefers it moist, ideal for typical autumnal weather, but may require a slightly sheltered position from harsh winds.

Schizostylis coccinea 'Major' produces large, silky, almost glossy, red blooms from late summer onwards held upwards on rigid stems and surrounded at the base with attractive, glossy foliage. It can seem surreal to see something appear that looks so exotic and tender flowering when all the usual stalwart, hardy plants are starting to fade towards the end of summer, and the flowers are also useful for cut flowers when there is little else left in the garden.

Suitable for planting near ponds and streams, but not actually in the water or boggy ground. In dry, sandy soil it will be necessary to add plenty of organic material. They also look good in herbaceous borders to create late autumnal interest, but may need protection with a mulch in the depths of winter if living in exposed or very cold areas.

Due to their rapid growth, plants may need lifting and dividing in spring to prevent them becoming too congested. Remove fading flowers to ensure they keep producing right into the depths of late autumn and early winter.

ALTERNATIVES
One of the most popular varieties is *S. coccinea* 'Sunrise', which is similar in size and habit to 'Major', but with salmon-pink flowers. An old garden classic is 'Mrs Hegarty', which originates from Ireland and dates back to 1921. This one is slightly smaller with pale pink flowers.

71

DAHLIA 'ORFEO'

ONE OF THE MOST RECOGNISABLE FLOWERS OF THE LATE SEASON BORDER, THE REPUTATION OF THE SHOWY DAHLIA HAS FLUCTUATED, YET IT IS ONE OF THE MOST USEFUL FLOWERING PLANTS, IGNORING THE SIGNS OF WINTER'S APPROACH UNTIL THE FIRST FROST.

When dahlias were first brought to Britain from Mexico it was as a substitute for the potato, with explorers hoping to make their fortune from the edible tubers. Fortunately, gardeners preferred to grow them for their flowers rather than eat them, and in the centuries that followed dahlia breeding reached a frenzy. The ease with which dahlias mutate and cross-breed led to ever bigger, more dramatic and showy blooms until eventually most could only be grown as specimens, too extreme in tone and form to fit alongside other plants in a border. Their star waned in the 1960s, and dahlias retreated to the plots and gardens of obsessional plantsmen and flower arrangers or found a place, miniaturised, in bedding schemes.

Luckily for modern gardeners, dahlias are having a comeback and it would seem the brighter and more garish the better. They fit in particularly well with sub-tropical or hot planting schemes where their vivid and lively appearance make them the perfect planting combination with plants with lush foliage or even grasses for providing late summer interest. One of the most popular dahlias is 'Orfeo' which is a purplish, red wine-coloured, cactus type that is also is a good choice for the cut flower border. .

All dahlias need rich, fertile soil with plenty of organic matter and water, and should be planted in full sun. If you are lucky enough to live in a very mild area, you can usually get away with leaving the tender bulbs in the ground over winter as long as they are well mulched, but for most of Britain it will be necessary to protect them against frost by lifting and storing them over winter. When the temperature drops too far the foliage will blacken almost overnight, making it easy to see that the time has come for them to be cut down and lifted.

ALTERNATIVES

Dark red cultivars such as 'Nuit d'ete' are velvety and rich, or try a hot pink like 'Hillcrest Royal' for real pizzazz. For those with more refined and subtle tastes, and who find most dahlias over-the-top and 'vulgar', they should try the more restrained Dahlia 'Bishop of Llandaff', which is probably the nations' favourite variety. It was bred in Wales, has truly outstanding good looks and is the kind of plant that compliments rather than overshadows everything around it.

72

CYCLAMEN
HEDERIFOLIUM

THIS LOW GROWING TUBEROUS PERENNIAL HAS IVY-SHAPED LEAVES WITH UNUSUAL MOTTLED PATTERNS OF SILVERY-GREEN ON ITS LEAF SURFACE APPEARING DURING THE WINTER MONTHS, WITH PINK, PURPLE OR SOMETIMES WHITE FLOWERS IN AUTUMN.

Love them or loathe them, the vivid, almost psychedelic pink flowers of ivy-leaved cyclamen, *Cyclamen hederifolium* is a real shock of a contrast to the traditional autumnal yellows, reds and oranges that appear on the berries, flowers and foliage at this time of year.

The pink flowers are a quirky, shuttlecock-like shape and have attractive, deep maroon flushed markings towards the base. An added bonus is that they are occasionally fragrant too. The flowers appear in autumn, usually before the winter foliage appears.

Although the flowers are very small, only about 2cm (¾in) across and the plants are very low, only reaching a height of about 12cm (4½in), they are not easily missed in the garden due to their vivid colouring. Once the flowers die back the plant leaves a beautiful, rich carpet of foliage. The leaves are shaped like ivy but have a mottled appearance of silver, grey and green. The mottling is very distinctive, and looks as if the shape of a Christmas tree has been stencilled onto each individual leaf. Planted in large clumps gives maximum effect.

They are very hardy and are best planted in dappled shade such as at the edge of a woodland or under shrubs and small trees, or alongside a hedge. However, they will also cope with sunshine and can be planted at the front of borders for an autumnal splash of pink colour. They're also suitable for planting in containers where their foliage can also be used as a foil for other planting combinations for winter and Christmas. They look great alongside ferns such as the native hart's tongue fern, *Asplenium scolopendrium*, and make a perfect backdrop among emerging winter aconites or snowdrops.

The best time to plant the tubers is in late summer about 2.5cm (1in) deep in well-drained soil. Add organic matter such as leaf mould to the soil prior to planting. Tubers should be about 10cm (4in) apart and quite a few of them are needed to maximise their impact.

They are practically maintenance free and they tend to look after themselves. They can benefit from a mulch of leaf mould once the leaves start to die back if they are grown in full sun, but if they're grown under deciduous trees, the falling leaves will provide the natural conditions they enjoy. They do seed freely however and rogue stray plants may need rescuing and planting in appropriate places in the garden.

ALTERNATIVES

The other commonly grown species of cyclamen is *C. coum*, which is another great choice for naturalising under trees and shrubs. The flowers appear later, from winter through to spring and they have a similar mottled pattern to *hederifolium* but on a kidney-shaped leaf.

73

NERINE BOWDENII

ONE OF THE MOST EXOTIC LOOKING FLOWERS IN AUTUMN WITH ITS BRIGHT, ROSE-PINK, TRUMPET-SHAPED FLOWERS WITH QUIRKY, WAVY-EDGED PETALS, HELD ALOFT ON THICK SPIKES, NERINE BOWDENII REALLY DOES ADD THE WOW FACTOR TO ANY FLOWER BORDER.

Flowering from late summer until late autumn, *Nerine bowdenii* is one of the best late flowering bulbs in the garden. Their attractive strap-shaped, mid-green leaves usually appear just after the flowers. An additional bonus is their faint musky aroma that scents the cool autumnal air. Being only about 45cm (18in) it is often the fragrance that I notice in the garden before seeing the plants in bloom.

The best place to grow them is in the herbaceous border where the bulbs can be planted in large blocks or rows to maximise their impact. This species was introduced by Cornish Bowden in 1903. They originate from mountainous areas of South Africa, and they like conditions to be similar to their native habitat which is dry and free draining. They often perform worse in wet and damp autumns. They also work well at the front of a hedge, so long as they're not in its shadow, where they can cope with the dry soil at its base. I like to see them growing by yew or other dark hedging where the flowers stand out better against the background. Their love of dry, parched conditions means they enjoy being planted at the base of a warm, baked, south-facing wall.

Bulbs should be planted just below the surface in mild areas although in cooler areas they should be planted about 5cm (2in) deep to ensure they don't get damaged by the frost. Plant them in late autumn or winter at about 10cm (4in) apart. Avoid digging in too much organic matter as this can cause lots of luxuriant foliage at the expense of flowers. Nerines generally prefer a light, free-draining soil. However, they will benefit from a layer of mulch being placed over the top of them after planting to protect them from frost.

ALTERNATIVES

There are about 30 different species but the only one hardy enough to grow outside other than *N. bowdenii* is undulata, which also has pale pink flowers with crinkly edges. One of the other famous nerines is the red or orange flowering *N. sarniensis*, commonly known as the Guernsey lily, from the seventeenth century when the bulbs were washed ashore from a passing ship and naturalised on the island. They are slightly tender and will only survive outdoors in frost-free gardens.

74 COLCHICUM AUTUMNALE

FORMING A RICH TAPESTRY OF DELICATE MAUVE FLOWERS ON THE AUTUMN GARDEN FLOOR, THE COLCHICUM IS EASY TO GROW AND A GREAT WAY TO LIVEN UP THE GARDEN AS THE DAYS BEGIN TO DARKEN AND SHORTEN.

Colchicums will grow in either dappled shade or full sun so are ideal for the edge of a woodland garden or underneath shrubs and small trees. They can be naturalised in the open lawn or alongside a hedge. They are also suitable for rock gardens where they enjoy the well-drained conditions and are great in containers or even window-boxes. If growing them in the lawn, do bear in mind that you will need to avoid mowing the lawn until the foliage has died back naturally in summer.

Confusingly, often called autumn crocus, although it is not actually a crocus, *Colchicum autumnale*'s other popular name is naked ladies because the flowers appear before the foliage, which appears during winter and persists into spring and summer. Even more confusingly, another common name is meadow saffron, although this isn't the plant that produces saffron – that is *Crocus sativus*.

Avoid heavy clay soil where possible and add plenty of sand or grit if these are the only gardening conditions available to you. Bulbs should be planted in late summer where they will quickly establish and grow quickly. If they spread too quickly they can be lifted and divided after flowering and redistributed in the garden.

The erect, strap-shaped leaves are up to 30cm (12in) in length and can look straggly for the remainder of the season so one trick is to plant them towards the back of a border, where spring and early summer herbaceous perennials will hide them until autumn when the plant in the foreground dies back or is cut back, revealing the naked ladies behind.

ALTERNATIVES
There is a gorgeous white form of *C. autumnale* called 'Album'. 'The Giant' produces huge, mauve-pink flowers but can spread rapidly. Another worth giving a go is *C. byzantinum*, which also produces lots of large, mauve-pink flowers or *speciosum*, which flowers later than autumnale so is a great way of extending the season. Another popular variety is *C.* 'Waterlily, which produces rosy-lilac petals.

75   CROCUS SATIVUS

THE HARVEST FROM THE SAFFRON CROCUS IS COMMONLY KNOWN AS
'RED GOLD' BECAUSE IT CAN BE MORE EXPENSIVE THAN REAL GOLD.
THIS BULB IS A STUNNER AND WILL ALSO PROVIDE YOU WITH YOUR
OWN SAFFRON SPICE TO USE IN THE KITCHEN.

These hardy bulbs deserve a spot in every garden. Appearing in early autumn *Crocus sativus* carpet the ground with their vivid purple flowers and bright red centres. Commercially they have been grown in the past to produce saffron and there are still a few enterprises growing them for this reason. It was a thriving industry in Britain and gave its name to the town of Saffron Walden.

The part that is harvested and dried to make saffron is the pretty central red filament that each crocus produces. However, before you start to see growing saffron in your garden as equivalent to winning the lottery, bear in mind that it takes up to 150 flowers to make a single gram of dried saffron. Considering each bulb only produces one or two flowers that represents a lot of back-breaking work for little reward.

Crocus is grown almost all over the world and so is suitable for most climates, but needs full sun. What it doesn't like is heavy soil. It requires light but fertile conditions, so if your garden is on clay, then you will need to add plenty of grit and sand to ensure the bulbs don't just rot in the soil. They can be grown at the front of flower beds for an early autumn splash of colour, planting them at 10cm (4in) apart and 7.5cm (3in) deep. Alternatively they can be naturalised in the lawn, by simply sprinkling the bulbs over the surface and planting them where they land at a depth of 8cm (3in).

ALTERNATIVES
C. kotschyanus produces very delicate pale pink flowers with pretty yellow centres and pure white stamens. The other popular autumn crocus is *C. ochroleucus* that appears later in the season and has pretty white flowers with egg-yolk yellow throats and stems.

76

VITIS 'BRANDT'

THIS SPECTACULAR GRAPEVINE LOOKS WONDERFUL WHEN ADORNING THE SIDES OF HOUSES OR DRAPED OVER PERGOLAS AND FENCES WITH WONDERFUL AUTUMN FOLIAGE. BUT EVEN BETTER, IT ALSO PRODUCES DELICIOUS GRAPES TO EAT OR MAKE WINE FROM.

Bring a touch of the rolling vineyards of France to your back door by growing this ornamental grapevine in your garden. *Vitis* 'Brandt' is a climbing plant and so will ideally need something to scramble up. My favourite place to see it is trained onto a pergola providing you with shade from the midday sun when dining al fresco during midsummer. As summer changes to autumn you can look upwards and see the grape bunches all hanging downwards, tempting to you to pluck them as they ripen. They are edible although there are better tasting varieties available, however, a reasonable wine can be made from them.

The main reason for growing this grapevine isn't for the fruit, but for the attractive, lobed leaves the size of dinner plates that turn a vivid red and purple as the cooler weather approaches.

Grapevines like a fertile, free-draining soil. They are usually trained as climbers on south-facing walls as they are real sun worshippers. However, if you're not worried about the grapes ripening, and just want the full-on autumn foliage effect, then partial shade will be fine. In smaller gardens they can be trained as fans or espaliers on a system of wires or trellis. They can even be grown as shrubs if regularly pruned. The best time to prune them is when the plants are dormant. Prune back all the new growth to two buds except, for the leading shoot, which can be trained in the direction you wish to grow it.

ALTERNATIVES
If you want to grow vines for wine, then you can go traditional by selecting chardonnay (for white wine) or pinot noir (for red wine), but you will need very favourable warm sites for them to ripen fully. Other, hardier varieties might be more suitable such as 'Muller Thurgau' (white grapes) but this is prone to mildew, or some of the modern varieties, such as 'Orion' (white grapes), 'Phoenix' (white grapes) or 'Regent' (black grapes).

77 PARTHENOCISSUS QUINQUEFOLIA

COMMONLY KNOWN AS VIRGINIA CREEPER OR AMERICAN IVY, THIS FOLIAGE-STUNNER PRODUCES DRAMATIC AND EYE-CATCHING RED AND CRIMSON LEAVES IN AUTUMN.

Originating from Eastern North America, this climbing vine is simply glorious when the temperatures drop and the attractive leaves turn fiery red and crimson. It is fair to say this climber is unrivalled in terms of impressive foliage. This is partly due to the impressive colours, but also due to the imposing size it can reach, producing a huge wall of intense autumnal foliage. To get the best colours it should be grown in full or dappled shade.

Possibly invasive if left to its own devices, be prepared to do the occasional radical prune. Once it starts to grow, stray shoots will need to be tied in, and others pruned back in autumn or early winter.

Due to its rampant growth it is possibly not always the greatest choice of plant for very small gardens or house-owners who are short on time and want low-maintenance gardens. Bear in mind they can reach as high as 20m (65ft), which can cause problems for plant care, particularly if they start to grow into gutters and brickwork.

Thriving in fertile, well-drained soil, the best time to plant one is in autumn when the soil is still warm.

ALTERNATIVES
P. tricuspidata, the Boston ivy, is similar to Virginia creeper but its leaves are three fingered instead of five. It too is a vigorous, self-clinging, deciduous climber with leaves that turn a shocking crimson and purple in autumn. Another similar choice is *P. henryana*, which has deciduous, dark velvety green or tinged bronze foliage.

PUTTING IT ALL TOGETHER

LARGE AUTUMN BORDER IN PART SHADE OR FULL SUN 6M X 2M

1. Acer palmatum 'Bloodgood'
2. Sambucus nigra 'Gerda'
3. Cotinus 'Grace'
4. Euonymus elatus 'Compactus'
5. Parthenocissus quinquifolia
6. Aster x frikartii 'Monch'
7. Penstemon 'Garnet'
8. Sedum spectabile 'Ruby Glow'
9. Kniphofia 'Royal Standard'
10. Dahlia 'Bishop of Llandaff'
11. Nerine bowdenii

This border will guarantee you a hot, fiery display of rich colour and tone as the season changes. Foliage colours in red, purple and black will provide a great backdrop to the late but dramatic dahlia and kniphofia flowers, while the gentler penstemons, asters and sedums provide cohesion and continuity.

● Allow *Parthenocissus quinquifolia* to climb the wall or fence at the back where its leaves will gradually turn deeper and deeper red.

● Plant the *Acer palmatum* 'Bloodgood' in the back left corner where it will receive most shelter from cold winds and the *Sambucas*

THESE AUTUMN BORDERS COMBINE STUNNING, LATE FLOWERING
BLOOMS WITH INTERESTING TEXTURES AND VIBRANT FOLIAGE TO
BRIGHTEN SHADY SPOTS.

nigra 'Gerda' in the opposite corner.

● *Cotinus* 'Grace' should be planted just off centre again towards the back to bring structure and a wonderful delicate tone to the scheme.

● Plant *Euonymus alatum* 'Compactus' in front of the Sambucus for colour contrast.

● Through the main part of the border drift, *Penstemon* 'Garnet', *Aster* x *frikartii* 'Monch' and *Sedum spectabile* 'Ruby Glow' interspersed with individual plants of *Dahlia* 'Bishop of Llandaff' for variety.

● Add *Kniphofia* 'Royal Standard' in the front corners and clumps of *Nerine bowdenii* at the front of this border to complete the effect.

AUTUMN PRAIRIE-STYLE BED IN FULL SUN 5M X 1M

A flat, relaxed scheme with only late flowering perennials can look extremely stylish. For extra interest grasses can also be added for a more textured effect. These are plants that need little care to perform well so this is a good scheme for those short of time.

❶ Helenium 'Moorheim Beauty'

❷ Aster x frikartii 'Monch'

❸ Sedum spectabile 'Ruby Glow'

❹ Rudbeckia fulgida var. sullivantii 'Goldsturm'

❺ Penstemon Garnet

● Plant several long skinny drifts of each flower, making sure that each drift overlaps at least slightly, for the most natural effect.

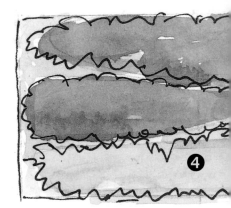

AUTUMN SMALL BORDER IN SHADE

Not all autumnal planting schemes have to be based on strong and vibrant colour. This small design is perfect for a shady area, where the white of the anemones and silver-leaved cyclamen will illuminate the gloom.

❶ Hydrangea 'Blue Wave'

❷ Anemone 'Honorine Jobert'

❸ Cyclamen hederifolium

● Plant *Hydrangea* 'Blue Wave' in the centre of your scheme with *Anemone* 'Honorine de Jobert' around its back and the tiny *Cyclamen hederifolium* scattered under and towards the front.

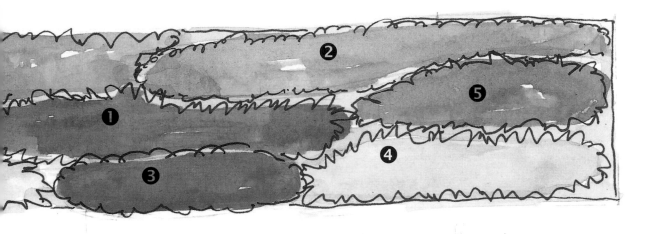

FEEDING YOUR GARDEN

Late autumn and leading into winter is the ideal time to get your composting area sorted as the garden starts to slow up and the craziness of spring and summer's growth is over. Having good compost in the garden helps to improve the quality of the soil and saves having to cart all your garden waste to recycling centres in the car.

Having a great garden isn't just about having great plants. It is also about trying to make it as sustainable and manageable as possible. One of the ways this can be done is to recycle all your garden waste into making good compost, which can then be added to the flower beds. You don't need a big garden for a compost site. There are small compost units that can be bought, such as daleks, that can be fitted into the smallest of areas. There are even some that have a rotating drum, so you don't have to physically turn the compost with a spade, but instead just turn a handle. They can easily be fitted into a corner in a courtyard garden or even onto a balcony.

For larger gardens, many compost heaps are made out of three pallets or fence panels, simply using

them on their edges, one at the back and two at the sides, nailed together. This very simple design is wonderful because it means it's easy to push a wheelbarrow in and out of the bay, and you can usually pick up pallets for free.

THINGS TO PUT IN YOUR COMPOST

Producing good-quality compost is all about getting the right balance. It should ideally be about 50 per cent nitrogen-rich material and 50 per cent carbon-based material. Compost should not be smelly or slimy, but should be nicely friable, crumbly and of a dark brown colour.

Nitrogen-rich material includes grass clippings, kitchen waste and other herbaceous materials. Carbon-based materials include newspaper, leaves and wood chippings. If you have too much nitrogen in your mix then the compost will go all slimy and stinky. Too much carbon and it won't break down.

To speed up the process of composition a compost heap should be turned every few weeks allowing the air to circulate around the material. When turning, all the material should be dug out of the heap and the stuff at the bottom put at the top ,and vice versa. Having an empty bay next to the current one to turn the compost into saves you having to double handle the compost.

If space allows you should have two or three compost bins on the go: one that is in use to add your material to; one that is in the process of decomposition; and a third one that is decomposed and ready to use in the garden.

Most fruit and vegetable kitchen garden waste can go into the compost, but avoid eggshells, meat and fish as they will attract rats.

It is useful to get a chipper if you can. Some of them are quite small and can be fitted into most sheds when not being used. They're great for getting rid of all those prunings. As well as adding into the compost, chippings can also be spread onto some of the beds to act as a mulch and help suppress the weeds. Wood chip is best used for around tree circles, beds in a woodland setting, shrub borders and around the base of hedges.

Leaf mould

In autumn, another useful material to use in the garden is leaf mould. This can be useful for putting around woodland plants as a mulch, as these plants are accustomed to having leaf litter falling around them in their natural environment. It can also be used for potting up shrubs, trees and ferns.

Making leaf mould couldn't be simpler. Simply gather up all the fallen leaves in the garden during autumn. Shred the leaves by running the lawnmower over them. Place them in a black bin liner, add some water (about a watering can amount) and leave somewhere dark and shady, such as behind the shed for it to rot down for a year. Next autumn you will have a lovely dark material to add onto the soil in your garden.

Comfrey and nettle feed

Plants will also enjoy a liquid feed to give them a boost during spring and summer, and this can be made for free from plant material. The two most commonly used plants are nettles and comfrey. Nettles are high in nitrogen and useful for feeding plants when they first come into growth in spring as it helps them develop lots of green lush leaves. Comfrey is particularly high in potassium, which helps plants develop flowers, colour and fruit set, and so can be used for feed later on in the season when plants start to come into bloom. However, both liquids do contain most of the essential nutrients required for plants so either will do if you just want to make one type.

● To make a liquid feed, cut back comfrey or nettles and collect up all the leaves.

● Fill up a bucket with the material and then cover it all with water.

● Leave it for a few weeks to allow all the material to rot down. Do be aware that this stuff really stinks so try to leave it somewhere where you won't be getting a whiff of it every time you step out into the garden.

● Once it has rotted down it needs to be sieved into plastic bottles.

● Feed plants once a week by diluting this concentrate at a rate of about 10 parts water to 1 part comfrey/nettle feed.

TREE PLANTING

Planting a tree is a long-term investment, so it is worth giving it the best possible start you can. Trees can vary in height enormously so check the details before purchasing to make sure you have room for it in your garden. To me, planting a tree is the most satisfying aspect of gardening. It is planting something of beauty that should hopefully survive for future generations. It is a way of enhancing nature while at the same time leaving your personal mark on the surrounding landscape.

Trees can be planted at any time of year, but the best time is autumn when the soil is still warm from the previous summer, and its roots will have time to settle into its new home before the onset of winter. Most trees come in containers (pots) but in autumn and winter bareroot trees become available, which are much cheaper and often healthier as they have been grown in the ground rather than in a pot, where they can become pot-bound.

The key aspect to planting a tree is to ensure it is not too deep. Many trees die in the first couple of years because the tree's trunk rots at the base from having been planted too deeply in the ground.

Step-by-step: planting a container-grown tree

● Dig out a circular hole that is double the circumference of the root system and the same depth. Place the spoil from the hole on a board to one side.

● Check the depth of the hole by placing the tree in the hole and putting a stick across it. The stick should be at the same level as the top of the rootball.

● Sometimes trees grown in containers have only recently been placed into their pots and therefore are deeper than they should be in the compost. Scrape back any loose compost at the base of the tree to reveal the top of the root system. That is the level the tree should be planted in the soil.

● Use a fork to spike the sides of the hole to encourage the roots to grow outwards rather than spiralling in the hole.

● Avoid digging and loosening up the soil at the base of the hole, because this will cause the tree to sink after planting. Only loosen the soil if there is a solid pan in the soil structure.

● If the tree is at the correct height, back fill around the root system using the spoil from the hole. If the soil is really poor it can be improved with compost, but ideally you want the tree to spread its roots outwards to find its own nutrients, as this will make the tree stronger and better anchored, rather than keeping its roots in the planting hole.

● Firm the soil around the roots, ensuring there aren't large air pockets left in the soil. The most effective way to firm it in the soil is to use your heel at the edge of the hole, with your toes pointing towards the trunk, and press down firmly, working your way around the tree. Afterwards check the tree is still upright and straight.

● If the tree is in an exposed position it will benefit from being staked to prevent it being rocked about in the wind. In sheltered positions the tree shouldn't need a stake. The stake should only remain for two or three years and then be removed as the tree should then have a strong enough root system to keep itself upright.

● Use a sledge hammer to bang a sturdy stake into the ground at about 45 degrees, ensuring you miss the rootball. Ideally the stake should be on the side where the prevailing wind won't keep blowing the tree onto it as this will damage the tree.

● Use a tree tie (or even a pair of old tights) to attach the trunk of the tree to the stake at about one-third of the way up the trunk. The idea is that the trunk further up will learn to flex with the wind and this will strengthen it enabling it to survive when the stake is taken away a couple of years later. Make sure the padding of the tree tie is between the trunk and the stake to prevent it from rubbing away the bark.

● Finally, water in the plant well and then stand back and admire your handiwork. Hopefully in years to come, you or even the next generations will also be able to stand back and admire it … albeit with a craned neck as they look at the heady heights to which it has now grown.

WINTER

THE COLD WEATHER can create a visual winter wonderland in the garden. Seedheads stand tall and resplendent, looking at their best when the winter frost catches them, making them shine and glisten in the winter sun. As temperatures drop and day length shortens, there is a warm pleasure from standing indoors with a hot mug of coffee or tea and admiring the structure of the garden from the comfort of your own living room or kitchen.

Trees and shrubs stand like sentinels defying the very worst that nature can throw at them. Only the toughest survive and some of them embrace it with such grace and beauty.

It's a time when the bare bones of the garden are revealed. Deciduous trees are denuded of their leaves and their gnarled, knotty branches create a new season of interest silhouetted against the backdrop of the low winter sun. Brightly coloured winter stems in an array of colours are provided by dogwoods and willows. Trunks with impressive textures or foliage stand out proud against the cold such as the papery, white bark of birch, the stripes of the snakebark acers or the deep red, mahogany and chocolate-brown of some of the cherry trees, which all create bold, upright features in the garden.

Wrapping up warmly with a woolly hat, thick socks, gloves and scarf are part of the ritual before stepping outdoors into the garden. Winter pruning is one of the main jobs in the garden and there is a wonderful satisfaction in shaping a bush or shrub to suit your own taste.

Many of the shrubs provide the chilly winter air with an intoxicating sweet fragrance such as daphne, mahonia, sarcocca, witch hazel and winter honeysuckle. Closer to the ground are the nodding heads of hellebores, while the evergreen foliage of ivy, some with brightly coloured variegated leaves, clothe walls and fences and carpet the ground.

For extra interest, don't forget the wildlife that will be attracted to your garden if you leave seedheads uncut and grow plants with bright berries. To give your feathered friends an extra hand to survive the cold winter you can always provide a bird table or feeders and a bird bath.

Previous page Mahonia at Winkworth Arboretum, Surrey.

Left Crocuses in The Courts Garden, Wiltshire.

78

Betula utilis var. Jacquemontii

THE STARK, PEELING TRUNK OF THIS BIRCH TREE FROM THE HIMALAYAS IS EXQUISITE. IT LOOKS GOOD ALL YEAR ROUND BUT IN WINTER, AS PURE WHITE AS THE DRIVEN SNOW, THIS SMALL TREE WITH ITS EXPRESSIVE STRETCHING LIMBS IS REALLY EYE-CATCHING.

Birch are one of the most commonly seen trees on the fringes of our many woodlands, happily colonising any space where a little bit of sunlight can filter through the higher canopy. Their ghostly, white trunks are a familiar sight in nature, but there are lots of garden varieties that have even more impressive and whiter trunks than those seen in the wild. One of the best forms is *Betula utilis* var. *jacquemontii*, Himalayan birch.

If space allows, grow them in groups of three or five where they make a much bigger impact. Try growing them against a dark backdrop, such as a yew hedge to get the maximum effect of their brilliant white trunks. At Greenway in Devon, we grow them against the backdrop of the dark River Dart to great effect, but they can equally be grown by the side of a pond in the garden, where the reflections will accentuate the trees. They can be underplanted with bulbs to emphasise the upright accents of the trunks. Snowdrops or snowflakes (*Leucojum*) are the best as they enhance the trunk's whiteness, but winter aconites, cyclamen or spring crocus are good alternatives.

In smaller spaces they can be grown in containers where they make all-year-round features in the garden. They can also be grown in raised beds where their elevated height shows off the trunks even more.

Birch trees aren't too fussy about soil conditions. They'll tolerate a range of pH conditions and will grow in clay or sand. They prefer full sun, but can be grown in dappled shade. They shouldn't require pruning except to remove any dead branches. You may want to cut off any really low branches to show off the trunk at its best. The tree will benefit from a mulch with well-rotted manure or compost at the base of its trunk, taking care to ensure the material isn't in direct contract with the trunk, to prevent it from starting to rot.

Birch can grow up to 12m (40ft) high but doesn't usually get to these heights in a garden. Birch are considered to be short-term trees, looking good for only about 25–30 years, and with the most impressive looking trunks when they're very young. This is opposed to trees such as oaks and yew that can live for hundreds of years. After a while, the intense white colouring of a birch tree can start to fade, and may be worth replacing. Some gardeners advocate going out each winter with a sponge and bucket of soapy water to wash off any algae and dirt on the trunk, ensuring that it looks sparkly clean.

ALTERNATIVES

For something more unusual try *B. utilis* var. *jacquemontii* 'Wakehurst Place Chocolate', which has a dark chocolate-coloured trunk. It makes a great contrast to the white stemmed birches if planted close together. *B. utilis* var. *jacquemontii* 'Grayswood Ghost' is regarded as having the whitest of any of the *B. utilis* var. *jacquemontii* cultivars.

79

ACER DAVIDII

DO YOU EVER WANT TO GIVE A TREE A HUG? I CAN GUARANTEE YOU WILL AT LEAST WANT TO GIVE THIS VERY TACTILE SNAKEBARK TREE TRUNK A STROKE EVERY TIME YOU WALK PAST, MAKING THE ACER DAVIDII A MUST FOR GARDENERS AND TREE-HUGGERS ALIKE.

How can anybody not be smitten with this tree from China? *Acer davidii* or Père David's maple has sumptuous green and white vertical stripes all up its trunk, often flecked with a whole range of other hues, such as dark reds, purples and browns. The beauty of this alone is enough to justify growing this tree, but it also produces attractive clusters of winged fruits and gives an impressive display of foliage flushed with orange, yellow and even pink leaves in autumn. Earlier in the year, this maple produces pendulous clusters of pale yellow flowers, which are very distinctive when examined close up.

It can be grown either with a single trunk or multi-stemmed, with the latter being the better option for drawing attention to its quirky snakebark texture.

Like most acers, *davidii* prefers sheltered locations away from exposed winds, but it is fully hardy and will tolerate the cold. They prefer partial shade, but will cope with full sun. They favour slightly acidic soil, but will cope with a moderate degree of alkalinity.

The best place to grow them is where their trunks can be seen at their best. So avoid planting them at the back of herbaceous borders or in amongst other plants that will screen its lower half when the plant is young. However, later on in life they can grow to about 10m (33ft) in height, which will lift the majority of the plant above the herbaceous foliage.

These acers make great focal points on lawns. Alternatively, in bigger gardens they can be planted at the edge of a woodland or on the margins of larger tree canopies, such as oaks, ash and pines. Woodland-type shrubs like camellias and rhododendrons make an attractive backdrop to acers with their evergreen foliage. Closer to the ground some of the small azaleas such as 'Greenway' look good near the base of the trunk. Snakebarks also look impressive when underplanted with low-growing ferns, winter aconites, snowdrops or *Cyclamen hederifolium*. They can be grown in large pots and containers, which is an ideal option for a small garden or courtyard.

ALTERNATIVES

The most commonly grown *A. davidii* is named after the famous plant hunter 'George Forrest', which has fantastic autumn colour and a fairly open habit. Another *davidii* variety worth looking out for is named after another explorer and plant hunter 'Ernest Wilson', which is more compact and considered by many gardeners to have one of the best displays of autumn colour. The variety 'Serpentine' is recognised as having one of the most ornamental bark patterns. Another snakebark species is *Acer pensylvanicum* from North America, which has impressive markings on its trunk and has attractive yellowy foliage in autumn. There are other acers that are grown for their ornamental trunk, with *Acer grisium* being the most popular, with amazing, golden coppery colours and a peeling, papery texture.

80

IF YOU THINK THAT ORNAMENTAL CHERRY TREES ARE ALL ABOUT THE BLOSSOM THEN THINK AGAIN. THERE ARE A NUMBER OF CHERRY TREES THAT HAVE GORGEOUS, COLOURFUL TREE TRUNKS THAT POSITIVELY SHINE WHEN THE WINTER SUN CATCHES THEM.

The deep, rich, mahogany-coloured trunk of *Prunus serrula* makes a bold statement in any garden. Creating an impressive feature all year round, winter is when the trunk stands out most prominently, almost radiating with a polished gleam. Striking, white, horizontal markings run up and down, standing out against the deep red colours, almost looking as if rich cream is spilling out from hundreds of lacerations. This deciduous tree from Tibet and western China forms a small, neat, rounded shape and is perfect for creating an upright, eye-catching focus point in a small garden.

The trunk can be 'buffed' or polished with a cloth to make it look even shinier, and remove any dirt or algae. Although its key attribute is the trunk, it also has attractive clusters of white cherry blossom in spring and mellow, yellow leaves in autumn.

Cherry trees require fertile, but well-drained soil. They absolutely hate wet, boggy ground and will instantly sulk as soon as conditions get too wet for them. In prolonged periods of dampness they often succumb to rot and fungal problems. In heavy clay soil it is worth adding a spade or two of grit to help improve drainage. In really poorly drained soil it may be necessary to grow them in large containers.

It is best grown as a multi-stemmed tree to make the most of its rich, coppery colours. However, it can also be grown as a single-stemmed tree, in which case it may be necessary to remove some of the lower branches to show the trunk off at its best. Planting should be in the autumn and should not be too deep, as this can cause the trunk to rot and the tree to die. The top of the rootball should be level with the ground or just very fractionally above it. Dig plenty of organic matter into the soil prior to planting to give the tree the best start in life. Young trees may need staking for the first couple of years until the roots have had a chance to anchor into the ground.

It is best not to prune a cherry tree where possible because they are so susceptible to disease. Only prune to remove any dead or diseased wood. This should be carried out when the plant is in growth, namely spring and summer. Avoid pruning in winter when the tree is dormant as the open wounds leave the cherry susceptible to fungal problems.

ALTERNATIVES
My absolute favourite is the slightly rarer *P. himalaica*, the Himalayan cherry, which has the most exquisite, rich brown trunk. A similar tree with a dark chocolate-brown trunk is *Prunus rufa*. For something a bit lighter *P. maackii* 'Amber Beauty' (Manchurian cherry) has glossy golden tones to its trunk.

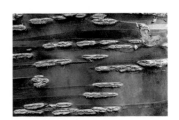

81 SALIX ALBA VAR. VITELLINA 'BRITZENSIS'

WHO SAYS THERE'S NO COLOUR IN THE GARDEN IN WINTER? THE VIBRANT, BRIGHT RED STEMS ON THIS WILLOW LOOK POSITIVELY ABLAZE AT THIS TIME OF YEAR, PROVIDING THE OUTDOORS WITH A BIGGER SPLASH OF COLOUR THAN ANY SUMMER FLOWER.

The young red stems on this shrub are so bright it looks like somebody has lit a bonfire in the garden. They look like burning, hot bushes and there is nothing quite like them for creating a maximum impact of colour outdoors.

Often referred to as the scarlet willow, the brightest colour appears on the new young stems. For this reason it is often coppiced or pruned to near ground level every one or two years. This is usually carried out in early spring, to cut the stems before it actively comes into growth to avoid loss of sap and also so you get to enjoy the colourful bare stems, denuded of their foliage throughout the whole of winter.

Although mainly grown as a coppiced shrub, they can be allowed to grow into an attractive tree, which can eventually reach about 10m (33ft) high and 15m (50ft) wide. Their leaves produce attractive green catkins in spring.

Like most willows they prefer moist soil. They will tolerate most other types of ground conditions except for extreme dryness. They are best planted by ponds where their long roots will thrive in the dampness and this means you get the added bonus of their colourful reflections. They're really tough plants and grow well in coastal and exposed locations. Pruning them once a year ensures lots of vibrant new stems to admire during wintertime with the entire plant covered in bright scarlet hues. They require sun or dappled shade.

ALTERNATIVES
There are numerous other willows with attractive winter stems so you can take your pick, but some of the most popular are *S. daphnoides* with intriguing violet stems. *S. x rubens* 'Eugenei' has pale, greenish yellow new growth and *S. alba x fragilis* produces fiery orange and red young shoots.

82

ILEX AQUIFOLIUM 'PYRAMIDALIS'

HOLLIES ARE ONE OF THE CLASSIC WINTER GARDEN PLANTS, PROVIDING EVERGREEN STRUCTURE WITH THEIR DARK, GLOSSY LEAVES AND A SPLASH OF COLOUR WITH THEIR BRIGHT BERRIES. ATTRACTIVE TO WILDLIFE, BIRDS LOVE FEEDING ON THE FRUITS.

I've had a love/hate relationship with many a holly in my gardening career. While I love the deep, glossy leaves and bright berries, I also remember the pain! Many a time I have cursed in the garden when I've been weeding without gloves (yes, I know I shouldn't) and inadvertently picked up fallen holly leaves and been stabbed by their prickly thorns. Thankfully *Ilex aquifolium* 'Pyramidalis' has far fewer prickles than some of the other varieties, which is a blessing.

'Pyramidalis' is so called because it has a lovely shape with a wide base and gradually tapers neatly towards the top. Hollies can be either male or female, but only the female ones produce berries. Thankfully 'Pyramidalis' is female and produces some of the brightest berries I have ever seen. It responds well to pruning so it is possible to keep it reasonably compact. Without pruning it will eventually make quite a large shrub, up to about 8m (26ft) in height and spread. Of course, clippings can always be used in Christmas wreaths.

Hollies are great for brightening up a dark, shady corner where not much else will grow because they tolerate shade and dry soil. They can also be planted in full sun and look great at the back of a deep border where their dark foliage provides a backdrop for low growing flowering plants with winter interest, such as periwinkle, hellebores, winter aconites or snowdrops.

ALTERNATIVES

If you want a prickly hedge as a barrier to keep out intruders then choose the very spiky *I.* 'Ferox Argentea'. For impressive foliage try 'Silver Queen', which has attractive variegated foliage with a creamy margin, although as it is a male (despite the confusing name 'Queen') it won't produce berries.

83 CORNUS 'MIDWINTER FIRE'

IF YOU ARE GOING TO CHOOSE ONE PLANT FOR MAXIMUM IMPACT IN A
WINTER GARDEN, THEN THIS SHRUB, LOADED WITH VIVID, BARE WINTER
STEMS IN FIERY ORANGES AND REDS, IS IT.

For about six or seven months of the year this
deciduous shrub is not particularly exciting to look at
with mid-green leaves and smallish, white flowers.
It becomes a bit more exciting just before leaf fall,
when the leaves turn an attractive orange-yellow,
but this dogwood really comes into its own when
the leaves drop off the tree in mid-autumn and
it continues to steal the show right up until mid-
spring. When its bare stems are exposed it creates an
unashamed riot of colour with its brilliant flame-
coloured stems.

Cornus are best planted *en masse* to maximise
their colourful, vibrant effect. In smaller gardens
plant them in clusters of three or five. They prefer
damp ground and look particularly effective next to
ponds where their reflections increase their bright
impression.

They prefer to be planted in full sun, and they also
look better because the winter sunshine seems to
accentuate their bright, bold colours. However, they
will tolerate dappled shade if necessary.

In order to get really colourful stems, it is best to
prune them hard, about 5cm (2in) above ground
level, in mid-spring, just before they come into
growth. Dogwoods will also benefit from a 5cm
(2in) layer of mulch around the base of the plant
to suppress any competing weeds and retain any
moisture.

ALTERNATIVES
One of the most popular dogwoods is *C.
sericea* 'Flaviramea', which has bright
lime-green winter stems, whereas *C. alba*
'Kesselringii' produces dark purple-black
stems in winter and has purple foliage all
year round.

84 HAMAMELIS X INTERMEDIA 'PALLIDA'

YOU MAY WELL SMELL THIS PLANT BEFORE YOU SEE IT, AS ITS SWEET, INTOXICATING FRAGRANCE CARRIES FOR LONG DISTANCES ON WINTER BREEZES. WHEN YOU DO SEE IT, THE SIGHT OF ITS ENCHANTING FLOWERS, LOOKING LIKE CANDIED SUGAR, WILL NOT DISAPPOINT.

This is probably one of my favourite winter shrubs, although I must admit to being partly biased as the original shrub originates from Battleston Hill at the Royal Horticultural Society Garden, Wisley, in Surrey where I previously worked as supervisor. I always used to love the smell every winter where its fragrance would dominate the scent on the hill in the fresh winter air. *Hamamelis* x *intermedia* 'Pallida' is one of the most popular hybrid witch hazels and reckoned by many to be one of the greatest of all the winter shrubs.

Witch hazels are deciduous and produce fragrant flowers on bare stems during winter before their hazel-like foliage appears. Later on in the year their leaves turn an attractive, buttery-yellow colour. 'Pallida' produces deep yellow flowers with amazing, bright reddish purple calyces.

It will grow up to about 5m (16½ft) in height and width if left unpruned and is fully hardy. In fact, one of the most exquisite ways of seeing the flowers is when they have been hit by a harsh frost and they look like frozen sweets suspended in the air. They tolerate full sun or partial shade and are not too fussy about soil conditions.

They can be planted as individual specimens and make eye-catching winter interest if planted in tree circles in the lawn, or look good planted among mixed borders, particularly those with bold foliage, such as acuba, mahonias, skimmias and hollies.

ALTERNATIVES

H. x *intermedia* 'Diane' is a popular orangey-red flowering variety. It isn't one of the most fragrant, but does have impressive autumn foliage. 'Arnold's Promise' has pretty, bright yellow flowers with bold autumn colour. 'Aphrodite' is another variety you could easily fall in love with that has large, fragrant, orangey-yellow flowers.

85 MAHONIA X MEDIA 'CHARITY'

EASY TO GROW AND UNFUSSY ABOUT WHERE IT IS PLANTED, MAHONIAS
PROVIDE PLENTY OF INTEREST IN THE GARDEN WITH THEIR LARGE,
EVERGREEN, GLOSSY LEAVES, DELICIOUSLY SCENTED FLOWERS AND
QUIRKY-LOOKING DARK FRUITS.

Like many winter flowering shrubs, mahonias have a delicious, sweet fragrance that carries on the fresh, cool air, attracting pollinating insects to feed from its nectar. A popular winter shrub, one of their best attributes is that they aren't demanding. They will tolerate sunshine, partial or full shade although they can get slightly leggy if they aren't receiving any sunshine at all. However, they do respond well to pruning, so if this happens, they can be cut back by half along the stem, where they will regrow, creating a more compact shrub. They're not fussy about soil conditions and will cope with almost anything except very wet or boggy.

They have glossy leaves, similar to holly but opposite each other on long, arching stems, which gives the plant a stately, architectural quality. Good for using as features in awkward areas, such as shady corners or under the canopy of taller trees, the sharpness of the leaves combined with their tough, hardy and dense habit, makes them handy shrubs for creating barriers from trespassers, or for screening unsightly areas of the garden. Mahonias are also useful plants for the back of the herbaceous border, with their distinctive leaves making a great background foil for lower growing plants and bulbs, such as hellebores, cyclamen and heathers in winter.

Mahonia x *media* 'Charity' is one of the larger types, growing to about 4m (13ft) in height and spread. It has an upright habit and pale yellow spikes of flowers that can be as long as 35cm (13in).

Later, it produces purple fruit that look like clusters of grapes, hence its common name Oregon grape. They require little maintenance, but will benefit from a mulch of well-rotted manure or garden compost once a year around the base of the trunk.

ALTERNATIVES
For something smaller try *M. aquifolium* 'Apollo', which only grows to between 45cm and 1m (1½ and 3ft) tall. It produces large, dark yellow flowers and black berries. *M. japonica* is slightly bigger than *aquifolium*, reaching up to 1.5m (5ft) high with long, leathery foliage and drooping flowers, compared to the upright spikes of 'Charity'.

86 VIBURNUM FARRERI

A DECIDUOUS SHRUB WITH GORGEOUS, CRINKLY LEAVES IS
COMPLEMENTED FROM LATE AUTUMN AND INTO WINTER WITH
CLUSTERS OF PERFUMED WHITE, PINK-TINGED FLOWERS.

The foliage goes through a whole plethora of
colours as the season progresses, starting off bronze
when young, then through to dark green and
finally a flamboyant flush of red and purple shades,
before taking their final bow in autumn. The pretty
clusters of whitish pink, tubular flowers appear in
late autumn and persist into winter with their sweet
scent perfuming the air.

They prefer moist but well-drained soil and will
tolerate sun or partial shade making it a versatile
plant in any garden. Although the plant is fully
hardy, the flowers can be prone to turning brown if
they get zapped by the frost so it is worth choosing a
sheltered site if possible. Discovered in north China
in the early twentieth century by the intrepid plant
hunter Reginald Farrer, it will grow to about 2.5m
(8ft) high and wide. Because of its delightful smell,
it can be a useful shrub to plant near the front door
where you will get a whiff of its fragrance every
time you go in and out of the house during winter.
It is often used as a hedge and can be trimmed once
a year after it has flowered to keep it in shape.

Viburnum farreri doesn't require much
maintenance, but like most shrubs, will benefit
from an annual layer of mulch being placed around
the base of its stems.

ALTERNATIVES
V. farreri 'Candidissimum' is a stunning, pure
white version of this species.

The other popular winter flowering
viburnum is the hybrid x *bodnantense*, which
produces clusters of pink, scented flowers on
its bare stems in winter.

87

Daphne mezereum

MASSES OF BRIGHT PURPLE, SCENTED FLOWERS APPEAR ON BARE STEMS FROM MID- TO LATE WINTER ONWARDS FILLING THE GARDEN WITH A SENSORY OVERLOAD OF FRAGRANCE. DAHPNE MEZEREUM IS A SMALL, COMPACT SHRUB MAKING IT IDEAL FOR SMALL GARDENS.

According to Greek mythology, Daphne was a beautiful waterside nymph who attracted the unwanted attentions of the god Apollo. Daphne appealed to her father for help, who turned her into a tree to protect her. Regardless of this legend, you can't help but fall in love with this shrub. Daphne may have been the daughter of a Greek god but her namesake really does smell divine!

Daphne mezereum is a hardy, winter flowering shrub that is grown for its sweet-perfumed flowers that appear in the tips of bare stems from mid- to late winter and persist until early spring. The flowers are a rich magenta colour and are followed by fleshy, toxic, red fruits. It prefers fertile, well-drained soil, which is neutral to alkaline. It is an excellent choice of shrub if your garden is on chalky ground.

They like to be planted in either full sun or dappled shade. It's a fairly compact shrub, usually only reaching just over 1m (3ft) high and wide. They're ideal for planting in a shrub or mixed border or on the edge of a woodland garden. Plant them in a sheltered spot as this helps the fragrance to linger in the air better. I have one planted at the bottom of my garden as it is a wonderful enticement to step outside on a cold winter's day to go and smell the flowers. Despite the shrub being quite a distance from my back door, I can usually smell it the second I take a step outdoors.

Maintenance is fairly low and the shrub is very easy to grow. They don't require annual pruning, but can occasionally have one or two of the older stems removed to encourage more young shoots as this is where the flowers appear. As with most shrubs, they will benefit from a mulch with organic matter, such as well-rotted manure or garden compost at the base of the plant. Spent mushroom compost is also a good mulch as it has a high pH.

ALTERNATIVES

D. bholua 'Jacqueline Postill' is an evergreen daphne, which is larger than *mezereum*, growing to a height of about 2.5m (8ft). It produces scented, pink flowers with white on the inside. *D. laureola* (spurge laurel) is another evergreen daphne with scented, pale green flowers and black fruit. Like *mezereum* it only grows up to about 1m (3ft) high. *D. odora* 'Aureomarginata' is an evergreen with variegated foliage with yellow edges. It produces reddish purple flowers in early spring and reaches a height of about 1.5m (5ft).

88

CHIMONANTHUS PRAECOX

A GRACEFUL, UPRIGHT SHRUB, WINTERSWEET IS GROWN FOR ITS
DELICATE, DEEP YELLOW FLOWERS AND THEIR SWEET FRAGRANCE,
WHICH APPEAR ON THE NAKED STEMS BEFORE THE LEAVES EMERGE.
IT'S A TOUGH PLANT THIS ONE, HARDY AT MINUS TEMPERATURES.

I love the flowers on wintersweet and it's worth getting close up to take a really good look. They have an outer petal, which is a gorgeous deep yellow colour, and then inside it is another one that has vivid flushes of reddish purple. They hang off the bare stems singly, in the depths of winter, as if to defy the cold weather outside. The leaves come out as the flowers fade, appearing opposite each other along the stem. They have a spicy aroma when crushed between the fingers.

For much of the year the shrub looks insignificant, and it might not be your first choice if space is at a premium. But it is well worth growing if you have the room, because the fragrance it gives off in winter is sensational, with an unusual concoction of sweet overtones and a spicy background. If you don't venture out into your back garden much in winter, then stick it out in the front, by the drive, along a path or near the front door as you will be able to enjoy the aroma every time you go outside. In larger gardens they can be placed at the back of flower borders or in a sheltered location next to fences and walls. Its slightly lax habit with arching stems makes it suitable for cottage gardens and informal settings. Given that the perfume is so different to the rose-like sweetness of other winter flowering shrubs, such as daphne, *Chimonanthus praecox* is best planted a little way away from others so that its uniqueness can be better appreciated.

Originating in China, where it grows in the mountain foothills at altitudes up to 3,000m (10,000ft), it was introduced into Britain in 1766 and has been a popular winter flowering shrub ever since. It grows up to 3m (10ft) high and 3m (10ft) wide, and makes a small, domed bush. It likes a well-drained soil and is quite happy in chalky, alkaline conditions. It prefers full sun and a slightly sheltered site; growing against a wall is a popular choice for gardeners in exposed or very cold areas, where it can be pruned once a year after flowering by removing shoots that are growing outwards back to a couple of buds, and training the ones that are horizontal and flush with the wall. Some of the older wood on over-congested bushes should be removed to allow space for new, young, arching stems. Wintersweet will benefit from a 5cm (2in) deep level of mulch at the base of each plant in early May.

ALTERNATIVES

There are two commonly grown varieties of *C. praecox*. Firstly 'Luteus', which as the name suggests, has completely yellow flowers, so none of the attractive purple flushes on the petals, but flowers slightly later than the species, making it a better choice if you don't venture outdoors in the depths of mid-winter. The other one is *C. praecox* 'Grandiflorus', which has larger leaves and the flowers are a deeper yellow, but possibly not such a powerful, spicy fragrance as the species.

89

LONICERA FRAGRANTISSIMA

FORGET ANY ASSUMPTION YOU MAY HAVE THAT HONEYSUCKLE IS A PLANT ONLY TO BE ENJOYED ON BALMY SUMMER EVENINGS AND TRY GROWING THIS WINTER BEAUTY FOR FRAGRANCE AND FLOWERS.

The honeysuckle family is far more diverse than one might imagine. As well as providing gardeners with one of the quintessential sights and scents of summer, *Lonicera* also includes quick growing hedging plants and ground cover and, of course, the wonderful *L. fragrantissima*, a winter flowering shrub that brings delicate spidery blooms and a heady perfume to the barest of garden seasons.

Planted near a sunny wall, close to a path, it will give you the perfect excuse to venture out into the garden even on the coldest days, to remind yourself of far off halcyon times. The stemless creamy white flowers festoon twiggy stems from Christmas onwards, emitting a delicious, redolent scent and enough nectar to tempt out thirsty bumble bees on mild winter days. The more sun it receives the more flowers it will produce.

Normally deciduous, though it may keep its leaves in mild areas, *L. fragrantissima* grows to around

2m (6½ft) tall but will spread wider, and can be cut back hard if necessary. In order to ensure plenty of flowers the following year any pruning should be done in early spring, just after the flowers have faded. Otherwise it can largely be left to its own devices as it is unfussy about soil and surprisingly drought tolerant.

ALTERNATIVES
L. fragrantissima is fairly ordinary when not flowering, but, if you can get hold of it, the cultivar *L.* x *purpusii* 'Winter Beauty' produces reddish purple young shoots to extend the season of interest into spring and early summer.

90 FATSIA JAPONICA

FATSIA JAPONICA BRINGS NOT ONLY A TOUCH OF THE EXOTIC TO
A SHRUB BORDER BUT ALSO MAKES AN EXCELLENT STRUCTURAL
EVERGREEN SHRUB WHERE SPACE IS LIMITED.

When *Fatsia japonica* was first brought to Britain
it was assumed to be tender and you may find older
books recommending it for a greenhouse display.
In fact it is perfectly happy in our winter climate as
long as it is not too exposed to cold north winds. It
will also do well in fairly shady conditions, where
other flowering shrubs would sulk.

The glossy, hand-shaped leaves are gorgeous, looking
like they belong in a rainforest, and they can grow
up to 50cm (20in) in size. However, branches are
relatively sparse so the plant is never overwhelming,
which makes it such a good choice for a small
garden. It will eventually reach a height of around
4m (13ft), but can easily be kept in check by cutting
back any long, unwanted stems. Its common name,
the false castor oil plant, is a reference to its foliage
shape and its resemblance to *Ricinus communis*, the
true castor oil plant.

Although it looks good all year round, *F. japonica*
is especially valuable in winter for the clusters
of black, shiny berries that follow creamy white
flowers held above the foliage. These look a little
like huge ivy flowers and are just as attractive to
late pollinating insects. As are the berries, which are
thoroughly enjoyed by blackbirds.

ALTERNATIVES
There is really nothing quite like *F. japonica*
that will flourish outside, however, for
gardeners with an interest in botany, its close
relation, x *fatshedera lizei* is a fascinating
hybrid of *Fatsia* and ivy, slightly smaller-
leaved but with a loose, climbing habit.

91 STACHYURUS PRAECOX

A SHRUB WHICH REALLY STANDS OUT BEAUTIFULLY IN THE DARK DAYS OF WINTER, STACHYURUS PRAECOX'S STRINGS OF FLOWER BELLS HANG FROM EVERY BARE BRANCH, LOOKING JUST LIKE CATKINS.

Stachyurus praecox is a wonderful winter shrub, worth hunting out even though it is not the easiest of plants to find. In full flower it is festooned with drooping, lemon-yellow flowers resembling tiny cow bells, each one joined to a central stem that can be up to 10cm (4in) long. They hang almost all the way along the bare, reddish bronze branches, as if someone has deliberately pinned them up to dry.

S. praecox needs neutral to acid soil to do well, which makes it an excellent shrub for woodland-style gardens, although it does require some sun at least and is best in dappled shade. In its native Japan it grows at the edge of the woods, a pioneer paving the way for bigger trees to march onwards and outwards. Given the right conditions it will eventually reach a height of around 4m (13ft), but may also spread by nearly the same amount. Fortunately it has a nice open habit so even when the leaves unfurl it is not overpowering.

It is pretty much hardy in Britain, although it is wise to provide some shelter from strong, chilly winds. Otherwise, as long as the soil is not too heavy, with a good mulch of leaf litter to hold in moisture it should be perfectly happy.

ALTERNATIVES
The *Stachyurus* family is limited and most are not necessarily hardy but the other possible variety to try is *S. chinensis*, even more difficult to find, but a little more delicate in leaf and flower, which will cope well in milder areas.

92 SARCOCOCCA HOOKERIANA VAR. DIGYNA

THE HONEY SCENT OF THE SWEET BOX, SARCOCOCCA HOOKERIANA VAR. DIGYNA IS A WONDERFUL SURPRISE GIVEN THE INCONSPICUOUS NATURE OF THIS UNASSUMING PLANT: SWEET, POWERFUL AND AS WARMING TO THE SPIRIT AS A HOT TODDY ON A WINTER'S DAY.

No commonly available member of the *Sarcococca* family could ever be called showy but they are lovely, useful little plants nevertheless. They will thrive despite most attempts to neglect them and tolerate a wide range of conditions, including difficult dry shade, a problem for most plants and most gardeners. They are ideal plants for shade in general, but can be grown in sun as long as the ground is naturally damp.

Sarcococca hookeriana var. *digyna* never grows too tall but will spread to around 2.5m (8ft) by suckers. Its evergreen leaves are a good, strong green that contrast well with the purplish stems. In winter the white flowers can hardly be seen, often hiding under the leaves but the scent they produce is unmistakeable, and they are then followed by glossy black berries that can remain on the plant for month after month.

S. hookeriana var. *digyna* is a perfect plant to grow in a pot near the door to make the most of the scent, but its real value lies in its tolerant nature, and it should always be first choice to cover a shady bank or slope where little else would grow.

ALTERNATIVES
For those with more space to fill, *S. confusa* grows to about twice the height of its smaller cousin and makes an excellent shrub for the middle of the border to provide evergreen structure throughout the year.

93 ERICA X DARLEYENSIS 'WHITE PERFECTION'

ALTHOUGH THE HEATHER FAMILY HAS A REPUTATION FOR PREFERRING ACID SOIL, ERICA X DARLEYENSIS HAS BEEN BRED TO THRIVE IN NEUTRAL CONDITIONS AND WILL EVEN TOLERATE A BIT OF CHALKINESS.

It is strange that mentioning the plant heather seems to conjure up two opposing images – the wild, ling covered moors, backdrop for so many passionate, tempestuous fictional relationships, stand in complete contrast to the neat tidiness of a suburban garden where heather and dwarf conifers are marshalled by loving owners. This only serves to show that the heather is a plant for many situations. It is also a useful plant in many other ways, having been traditionally employed for bedding, fuel, cloth dye and making wonderful honey.

The acid-loving heathers tend to flower in the summer. *Erica* x *darleyensis* is different not only in its tolerance for less acidic conditions, but in its flowering season, making it a valuable addition to the garden in early winter. Given good soil that does not dry out too much it will perform well, not only smothering weeds but covering itself entirely in pretty-coloured, bell-shaped flowers. It needs only a light trim to remove any dead flowerheads and will then produce plenty of pinky cream new growth through the summer months.

E. x *darleyensis* 'White Perfection' is generally considered to be one of the best ericas available, with pure white flower spikes and strong foliage. It is spreading in habit rather than tall, reaching about 40cm (16in) in height, and has deep green foliage that turns a slight bronze in the winter months.

ALTERNATIVES
E. x *darleyensis* 'Phoebe' is a pretty salmon colour, compact and perfect for a smaller space or a pot display.

For extra height the award-winning *E.* x *darleyensis* 'Kramer's Rote' and its cultivated varieties is an excellent choice.

94 ERANTHIS HYEMALIS

CARPETING THE WOODLAND FLOOR IN A VIVID, BRIGHT YELLOW COLOUR, WINTER ACONITES ADD A WARM GLOW AND ARE A WELCOME SPLASH OF COLOUR DURING SOME OF THE COLDEST AND DARKEST MONTHS OF THE YEAR.

Closely related to the buttercup, but far more attractive, is the pretty winter aconite. They produce bright yellow flowers upon a ruff of green, deeply divided flower bracts. Originally a woodland plant from Italy and southern France, they send out a flush of tulip-shaped flowers from mid- to late winter. Plant them under deciduous trees and shrubs to replicate their natural growing conditions. In the wild they flower, grow and seed all before the canopies of the overhead trees come into leaf, meaning they can maximise the sunlight during their small lifecycle above ground, while enjoying shelter from the larger trees. At Polesden Lacey in Surrey where I was garden manager we had masses of *Eranthis hyemalis* in the classic Graham Stuart Thomas designed Winter Garden, growing under three large Persian ironwood trees. They only reach about 10cm (4in) high and so need to be planted in large quantities to really make an impact.

Tubers should be planted in autumn and they prefer fertile, moist, but well-drained soil. They will freely seed themselves. If they become too congested they can be lifted while 'in the green', which basically means while still in leaf, and moved. Propagating them is easy too; simply dig up the tubers after flowering and cut them into smaller sections, before replanting. Like many bulbous plants, avoid cutting back their scruffy foliage after flowering as they need to continue growing to store energy for the following year. By mid-spring the foliage should have died down naturally.

ALTERNATIVES
There are a few rarer cultivars to try such as *E. hyemalis* 'Guinea Gold' with bronze green foliage and 'Orange Glow' with slightly deeper coloured flowers. There is also a double flowering one called 'Flore Pleno', which needs sheltered, shady locations to thrive. *E. hyemalis* 'Cilicica Group' is another popular variety with larger flowers and finer foliage.

95

BERGENIA
'BALLAWLEY'

GLOSSY EVERGREEN LEAVES THAT COVER THE GROUND ARE NOT ALL THE BERGENIA HAS TO OFFER IF YOU CHOOSE THE RIGHT VARIETY. THERE ARE FLOWERS IN SPRING AND OCCASIONALLY AUTUMN, AND RICH WARM TONES THAT GLOW AND SHINE IN THE WINTER MONTHS.

Bergenia, sometimes called 'elephant's ear', is a plant commonly recommended as ground cover for shady areas but this pigeonholing does it an injustice, condemning it to the darkest, gloomiest place in the garden and to mere workhorse status. Admittedly it is a very unfussy plant indeed, happy in all kinds of soil and situations except extreme dry heat, and the evergreen tough leaves do a wonderful job of denying light to any weeds trying to grow under them. However, that is by no means the end of the story.

In a way bergenia is almost two plants. Give it moist, rich soil in sun or partial shade and it will put on plenty of glossy, new, attractive growth and flowers in spring, but in poor soil and an exposed site it will put on a completely different type of display, equally rewarding at a time when choices are limited.

In the colder, frostier conditions of winter, the foliage of many bergenias will colour up wonderfully, with tones ranging from scarlet through burgundy almost to purple. Many of our greatest garden designers have made the most of this, bringing bergenia out from under its bushy hiding places and placing it at the front of the border or display. Here it takes its place as a great plant in its own right, chosen for its winter leaf change or as a vibrant backdrop to plantings of snowdrops and other early bulbs.

Bergenia 'Ballawley' will give you the best of both worlds. The largest of the bergenias, its pink flowers stand 60cm (2ft) tall, flowering in both late spring and to a lesser extent again in autumn. The extra-large leaves will then turn a rich, red bronze. Like all bergenias it requires very little attention, needing little more than the occasional removal of dead material and can be increased simply by cutting off some of the fleshy rhizomes for replanting.

ALTERNATIVES

If the bold structural statement of *B.* 'Ballawley' is a little too much for you then *B.* 'Baby Doll' might be more to your liking. At only 18cm (7in) high its pink flowers and smaller foliage provides a more delicate show. For maximum winter colour *B.* 'Eric White' is an excellent choice. Its upright leaves turn deep red, almost black and are simply gorgeous.

96

HELLEBORUS X HYBRIDUS

ONE OF THE BEST FLOWERING PERENNIALS FOR THE WINTER GARDEN, HELLEBORES PRODUCE LOVELY, SAUCER-SHAPED FLOWERS FROM AS EARLY AS DECEMBER, ALL THE WAY THROUGH TO APRIL DEPENDING ON THE SPECIES.

Their beauty and flowering season have earned them the names 'Christmas rose' and 'Lenten rose'. Hellebores in general flower just after Christmas in a wide range of colours, from white through to the deepest purple-black, although the darker, smokier colours are usually the most desirable. Occasionally they have added spotted patterns.

The offspring of the oriental hellebores are notoriously variable, so just letting them self-seed around your garden could bring you some surprises, although the flowers themselves are always uniformly attractive whatever their eventual colour. It is always worth keeping an eye on the seedlings to see what may actually appear. Oriental hellebores, especially, are so variable that they are often sold by colour and type rather than by named varieties.

The evergreen leaves have a very distinct shape and are tough enough to survive snow without a problem, doing a wonderful job of protecting the unfurling flower buds. It is worth remembering that these older, overwintering leaves are best cut back just before the flowers open or they will continue to hide the delightful, outward-facing blooms. The new season's leaves will appear soon enough.

The best spot to plant hellebore is under the canopy of deciduous trees, so that the flowers get the maximum amount of any available winter sunshine while enjoying cooler, shadier conditions in the summer months. This will also help shelter them, as they dislike being exposed to drying winds and will do less well in open, harsher sites.

Woodland conditions also guarantee their soil needs are met. Rich soil with plenty of leaf mould or other organic matter will be perfect, as long as it is not too acidic.

ALTERNATIVES

The plant usually called the Christmas rose is *H. niger*, a compact plant with blue-green leaves and pure white flowers that sometimes fade to pink as they age. It is smaller and a little better behaved than its oriental cousin but nevertheless a wonderful sight. For sunnier, more exposed conditions try the Corsican hellebore, *H. angustifolia*, with its spiky, silver-green leaves and green flowers. It packs quite an architectural punch.

97 GALANTHUS ELWESII

THERE IS NO SIGHT THAT CHEERS THE HEART MORE THAN THE SNOWDROP NUDGING UPWARDS THROUGH THE FROST AND SNOW OF LATE WINTER, FOLLOWED BY A MULTITUDE OF DELICATE, NODDING BELLS. MINIATURE PERFECTION WITH VERY LITTLE EFFORT.

The humble snowdrop is one of our best-loved plants and one of the easiest to grow, requiring little more than a well-drained soil with plenty of leafy mulch. This makes it ideal for planting under deciduous trees, where there is plenty of springtime light before the canopy unfolds, and dappled, cooling shade in the summer months. Not that the snowdrop necessarily requires shade as such. Try planting them on a north-facing bank and they should thrive, with the added advantage of being a little easier to examine closely without getting down on one's hands and knees.

All snowdrops are tiny plants, normally reaching little more than 15cm (6in) high at most, but *Galanthus elwesii* is almost a giant in comparison to the others. At around 30cm (12in) tall it makes for a surprisingly dramatic display when planted *en masse*. The leaves are relatively broad for a snowdrop but it is the flowers that make this plant so special. The three outer sepals seem to open wider than others and their length and shape are reminiscent of moth wings, while the inner flower has emerald spots, which contribute to the effect of a silky-winged insect at rest. They are absolutely fascinating to look at and, to add to the attraction, also have a definite honey scent.

G. elwesii are perfectly hardy and the flowers are amongst the earliest to appear so a drift of these is almost certainly guaranteed to appear each year. Like other snowdrops they are easily increased by digging up congested clumps as soon as the flowers are over and replanting sections 'in the green'. This garden term simply indicates a bulb planted while it still has green leaves and is generally thought to be the most successful way of spreading snowdrops out. Having said that, *G. elwesii*, coming from the mountains of Turkey with hot, dry summers, can tolerate drying out after lifting and survive. Keep lifting and dividing this way and you will end up with a carpet of nodding white bells.

ALTERNATIVES

Lovers of the snowdrop have a wealth of cultivars and types to choose from, thanks to their natural tendency to change and the tireless efforts of breeders. *G. nivalis*, the common snowdrop, is always a perfectly good choice for large-scale planting drifts, either under trees or even in grass, but there are many, many fancier snowdrops to be found from specialist nurseries, including yellow-marked, double and upward-facing flowers, and even an autumn flowering snowdrop.

HEDERA 'BUTTERCUP'

CLIMBING IVY, THE DARK GREEN LEAVES THAT CLOTHE OUR WALLS AND ABANDONED BUILDINGS, WILL BE FAMILIAR TO MOST, BUT SOME MEMBERS OF THIS FAMILY, LIKE HEDERA 'BUTTERCUP', HAVE A MORE CHEERFUL EFFECT AND CAN PERFORM A DIFFERENT FUNCTION.

One of the few plants that can cope with dense, dry shade, ivy is usually recommended for places where no other plant could survive. Although officially a climber for trees, walls or unsightly objects, it is also much used in gardens as ground cover, since most varieties are as happy growing horizontally as they are vertically and its trailing habit can also be utilised in pots and planters. In effect the long tendrils of ivy have one purpose and one purpose only, which is to cover bareness, wherever it finds it.

The standard dark green ivies provide a good background for lighter planting schemes, making an excellent substitute for yew hedges in smaller gardens, and surviving where yew could not. As long as ivy is kept away from house gutters and eaves and lightly trimmed once a year it will rarely be a problem. The aerial roots that it uses to attach itself do no permanent harm.

It is worth remembering though that there is a noticeable difference between juvenile ivy, with its defined leaves and tendrils and its mature, flowering form, which will appear if ivy is left to grow unfettered. When mature the leaves broaden and become less shapely, the growth bushes out in all directions and in late summer cream flowerheads appear that are a magnet for flying insects of many types, followed by the black berries that are loved by birds. Mature ivy is one of the best wildlife attractors of any garden, providing shelter and food for any number of creatures but its weight and the restrictions on cutting it in the bird nesting season make it a little more problematic to live with.

Few such issues surround *Hedera* 'Buttercup', however, as long as it is planted in a sheltered position. Growing only to around 2m (6½ft) high, *H.* 'Buttercup' is much more manageable, and it will bring not Gothic gloominess but sunshine brightness to your walls. This is a plant that really deserves to be centre stage. Indeed planting it in the background in shade would be a pointless exercise as its glorious yellow leaves need sun at least some of the time to keep their colour. It is a perfect choice for a city garden or a courtyard, preferring chalky soil but tolerating a wider range of conditions happily.

ALTERNATIVES
H. colchica has the largest leaves and is an excellent choice for ground cover in difficult places. In pots, especially for winter displays, small-leaved ivies, such as *H.* 'Garland' can be allowed to trail over the edge.

99 CLEMATIS CIRRHOSA VAR. PURPURESCENS 'FRECKLES'

IF YOU ARE PREPARED TO PROTECT THIS WONDERFUL PLANT FROM THE WORST OF THE WINTER WEATHER YOU WILL BE REWARDED WITH ONE OF THE MOST DELIGHTFUL WINTER FLOWERING DISPLAYS IMAGINABLE. PURE MAGIC.

Gardeners are fortunate to have such a wide variety of clematis to choose from, providing flowers almost the whole year round. Although the big summer clematis are the most familiar and popular, *Clematis cirrhosa* var. *purpurescens* 'Freckles' has a charm that can supersede all of its showy cousins and is all the more welcome in a garden at a time when so little else is available. This clematis is festooned from late autumn right the way through to early spring with delectable speckled blooms and silky seedheads.

Its evergreen leaves become slightly bronze during the winter months and make a superb backdrop to the four-petalled flowers that start off as creamy yellow bells before opening up and showing off their maroon speckles. The overall effect is reminiscent of butterfly wings. As the flowers are followed by wispy, silky seedheads, there is always a fairy lightness to this plant that makes it irresistible.

In mild areas this clematis needs only the shelter of a north wall and to enjoy as much warmth as the winter sunshine can provide. In colder areas it is probably best grown in a pot so that it can be brought inside when harsh weather threatens.

Otherwise it is perfectly happy in fertile, neutral to chalk soil, where it should be planted, unlike many other clematis, at the same level as its surroundings. If you can shade the roots with another plant it will perform even better.

Pruning is also less tricky than for other clematis. In late spring, after flowering, simply remove any dead or damaged stems as required. Untangling is usually a waste of time and the plant is better cut back completely almost to the ground every now and again if control is needed. It will reshoot quickly and should then be left for at least three years before performing such drastic surgery again.

ALTERNATIVES

There are other *C. cirrhosa* available to try. *C. cirrhosa* var. *balearica* is the Majorcan original and has more muted, lighter spotting that produces a slightly antiqued effect, while *C. cirrhosa* 'Wisley Cream' has no markings at all, just creamy, elegant flowers.

JASMINUM
NUDIFLORUM

JASMINUM NUDIFLORUM IS ALWAYS ONE OF THE FIRST PLANTS OF
THE YEAR TO COME INTO FLOWER, PRODUCING ITS BUTTER-YELLOW,
FLARED TRUMPETS ALL ALONG ARCHING BARE STEMS OF BRIGHT
GREEN. ONLY AFTER FLOWERING DOES IT PUT OUT ITS LEAVES.

I adore this sprawling shrub, the winter jasmine, and thankfully where I live on the south coast I see it everywhere. In the sandstone walls of South Devon seaside towns, this plant can often be found cascading out of nooks and crannies where one could hardly believe anything could grow, let alone a shrub wreathed in bright yellow flowers in the middle of winter.

It is completely hardy, vigorous and very easy to grow, requiring very little in the way of fertility, hence its ability to grow out of walls or on cliff faces with shallow soil. This makes it a very useful plant for covering a steep bank, where its cascading effect will be at its best and its cheerful brightness a welcome relief during dark winter days. It is also a useful plant to train up a trellis or wire, although its natural habit is always to arch outwards, so if the idea of controlling does not appeal try growing it naturally over a low wall instead.

Jasminum nudiflorum needs the occasional trim, removing weak stems and leaving the stronger growth, and it is beneficial, though not essential, to remove a few of the older stems each year to encourage new growth from the base to keep the plant fresh.

ALTERNATIVES
There are no hybrids or cultivated varieties of winter flowering jasmine but you could substitute the shrub *Coronilla valentina* subsp. *glauca* for a more substantial effect within borders where *J. nudiflorum's* arching habit would be unsuitable. The pea-like, yellow flowers are fragrant and also arrive in winter and early spring on a bushier shrub with blue-grey leaves.

PUTTING IT ALL TOGETHER

ELEGANT LARGE WINTER BORDER 6M X 2M

1 Betula utilis var. jacquemontii

2 Ilex aquifolium 'Pyramidalis'

3 Clematis cirrhosa var. purpurescens 'Freckles'

4 Helleborus x hybridus

5 Erica x darleyensis 'White Perfection'

6 Bergenia 'Ballawley'

7 Eranthus hymenales

8 Galanthus elwesii

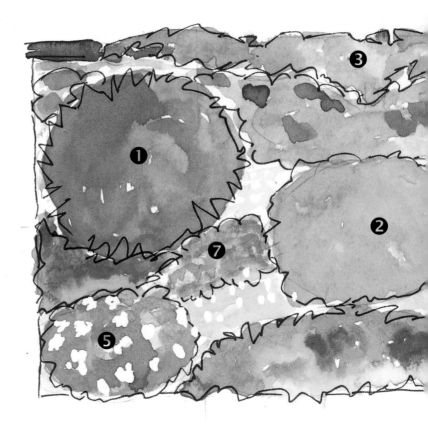

A winter border can look extremely elegant if the right plants are chosen, especially those that will shine through low light levels. In this design the glossy dark greens of the *Ilex aquifolium* 'Pyramidalis' and the leathery hellebore leaves are a foil for the white trunks of the Betula utilis and the *Galanthus elwesii* underplanting.

● Plant and train *Clematis cirrhosa* var. *purpurescens* 'Freckles' up the wall or fence on the left side.

● Plant one *Betula utilis* at

A WINTER GARDEN CAN BRING AS MUCH JOY AS THE FIRST FRESH, BRIGHT BLOSSOMS OF SPRING. THESE BORDER IDEAS COMBINE STUNNING COLOUR WITH INTENSE FRAGRANCE FOR AN ALL-ROUND SENSORY EXPERIENCE.

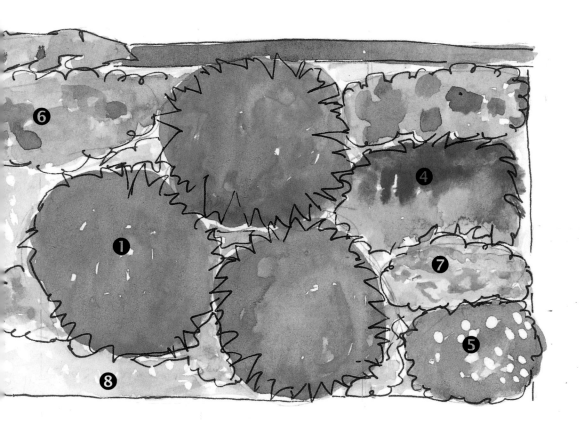

the back left of the border and another three towards the right. In between plant the *Ilex aquifolium* 'Pyramidalis' where its shape will not be impeded by other plants. At each of the front corners place *Erica* x *darleyensis* 'White Perfection' to add some low structural interest.

● *Begenia* 'Ballawley' can be planted in drifts along the back of the border with clumps of Helleborus x hybridus and Eranthus hymenales in front. Any remaining space can be filled with Galanthus elwesii.

KIDNEY-SHAPED BED IN FULL SUN

With winter sunlight filtering through the planting, this kidney shaped bed will glow and bring real joy and colour to your winter garden. Both the *Salix* and *Cornus* will need hard pruning in spring to ensure that their stems remain colourful.

❶ Prunus serrula

❷ Cornus 'Midwinter Fire'

❸ Salix alba var. vitellina 'Britzensis'

❹ Erica x darleyensis 'White Perfection'

● Plant *Prunus serrula* with its lovely bark to the right of your bed, then add clumps of *Cornus* 'Midwinter Fire' towards the centre and *Salix alba* var. *vitellina* to the right. Edge the bed with *Erica* x *darleyensis* 'White Perfection' for structural contrast.

SMALL SCENTED BORDER

If you have space outside a window or door this small grouping of scented plants is guaranteed to bring you pleasure without venturing too far in cold weather.

❶ Mahonia x media 'Charity'

❷ Daphne mezereum

❸ Sarcococca hookeriana var. digyna

● Plant *Mahonia* x *media* 'Charity' on the right hand side. Add *Sarcoccocca hookeriana* var. *digyna* at the front and *Daphne mezereum* on the left hand side.

WINTER PRUNING

Pruning a plant can be very satisfying. It may seem harsh, to stand there in winter wielding a pair of secateurs, loppers or a saw and start removing some of the limbs of a tree or shrub. However, very often the plant will benefit enormously from this 'surgery' and it should encourage the plant to flourish for years to come.

There are numerous reasons why it may be necessary to prune a tree or shrub:

1. Pruning can give the plant better shape. Some trees and shrubs get leggy and lose their structure. Sometimes it can be a specific shape, such as with topiary; at other times trees are merely pruned to keep the tree looking balanced.

2. Pruning reinvigorates a tree. So if you have a spindly tree that isn't growing well, it may be encouraged to put on more growth if it is pruned. Very often by pruning the tip of a shrub back by about a third, it will encourage more laterals (side shoots) to grow. This is often done on fruit bushes to encourage more fruiting shoots.

3. Pruning helps to improve the circulation of air around a tree or shrub. If a tree's branches are really congested it can cause fungal problems due to poor air circulation and a build-up of both pests and diseases.

4. Trees with ornamental trunks, such as birch and *Prunus serula*, look better if the lower branches are removed so that it can be seen more easily. This process is called crown lifting.

5. Plants that have colourful winter stems like cornus or willow can also be pruned down to near ground level to encourage a plant to send out more colourful stems. This is usually done just before the plant

comes into growth in late winter. Some plants, such as hazel and sweet chestnut are also often pruned in this way to encourage young, new, straight stems that can then be harvested later and be used for plant supports and stakes. This process is called coppicing. Some trees are pruned higher up the trunk, in a technique called pollarding.

6. It can improve better fruiting or flowering. For example, roses or wisteria are often pruned in late winter as this encourages more flowers for the following year. Fruit trees will nearly always fruit more if pruned. Do remember, though, that most of the stone fruit family (plums, cherries, damsons, peaches, apricots etc.) should only be pruned when in growth (so not winter) as it can cause disease to enter the plant.

7. Sometimes it is necessary to prune a plant for the benefit of a neighbouring plant. For example, if a tree has outgrown its space and is casting too much shade over its surrounding area, it might be preventing plants nearby from growing properly.

8. To remove dead, dying or diseased branches. If these aren't removed they can become a source of infection and the infection can spread to the remainder of the tree.

Tools of the trade

Secateurs are the essential tool for pruning. The best type of secateurs are bypass types that have a cutting action similar to scissors. They give the cleanest cut without damaging the plant. Anvil-type secateurs are the other poplar type whereby one blade comes down onto another. These are fine, but can cause the remaining wood to become crushed, which can lead to infection.

Loppers are useful for cutting larger shoots. Some of the more expensive types have a ratchet system that helps you get through the really thick stuff.

Pruning saws are used for the largest branches. They are designed so that they can fit into small spaces and help you get a clean cut. Some are folding types, which are really useful for carrying around in your pocket when out and about in the garden.

Step-by-step: pruning for winter colour

● Prune dogwoods in late winter or early spring each year just before they come into growth. Start by removing any damaged or diseased shoots.

● Next, look to remove any weak or wispy growth to make the plant look tidier.

● Prune back the new growth on remaining larger shoots to about two buds from the base of the plant. These are the ones you want to shoot out and provide the winter interest next year.

● Remove some of the gnarly old stems and spurs at the base of the plant because if they all send out shoots then the winter stems will look messy and tangled.

MAINTAINING THE GARDEN

Enjoying gardening is not just about choosing and planting our favourite plants. They all need some looking after, even the low-maintenance ones. However, looking after them is just as rewarding as planting them. It gets you outside in all kinds of weather, enjoying the wildlife, getting pleasure from making your hands dirty, and getting up close and personal with those plants that you put in the ground for fun.

Weeding

Whether we like it or not, one of the most common jobs in the garden is weeding. In fact during the spring and summer it can seem like that is all you're doing in the garden. The best method of reducing the amount of future weeding is 'prevention'. Avoiding having bare soil is the key, because wherever there is exposed ground weeds will quickly colonise it. Ideally empty beds should be planted up with exciting new plants, but if this isn't possible then they can be covered with weed-supressing membranes or a natural mulch, such as well-rotted manure or garden compost until it can be planted up.

The reason for removing weeds is not just because they can look unsightly, but also because they compete with your existing plants for nutrients and water in the soil. Some weeds get so big that they will also swamp and smother the plants, blocking out light and preventing them from growing to their full potential.

There are essentially two different types of weeds, annuals and perennials. The former are usually easier to control and spread by seeding everywhere.

Some of them will pull easily out of the ground by hand; others can be removed by hoeing. Ideally try to remove the weeds before they form their seedheads and start spreading everywhere. Annuals can be left to desiccate on the surface after hoeing in warm, sunny weather. Otherwise they can be raked up and added to the compost heap.

Examples of annual weeds: fat hen, annual meadow grass, chickweed, groundsel, annual nettle, hairy bittercress.

Perennials are far harder to control as they have pernicious root systems that lie beneath the surface of the soil. All the roots of these plants need removing to eradicate them completely. That's not always an easy task considering that some roots can be several metres below the surface. To make matters even worse, unless the plant with all its root is removed, it can still spread if added to the compost heap immediately. Perennial roots should be bagged up and removed, or they should be left out to dry in the sun for a few weeks before finally being added to the compost.

Examples of perennial weeds: bindweed, ground elder, knotweed, perennial stinging nettle, dandelion, brambles, *Equisetum* (mare's tail).

Opposite above left Always clean tools after use and wipe blades with an oily rag.

Opposite above right Stay on top of weeds otherwise they could take over your garden.

Opposite below A hoe is excellent for getting rid of annual weeds but will leave the roots of perennials in the ground.

ADDITIONAL INFORMATON

Types of plants

Evergreen plants

Evergreen plants retain their leaves all year round and are essential design elements in a garden as they provide permanent structure and interest within planting schemes. They can take many different forms, from huge redwood conifers stretching up to the sky to sprawling ivy covering the ground. They can be intricate ferns in a shady border or hellebores in a flower bed. Some of the larger trees and shrubs can be used as hedging, as screens or simply to create a bold statement with individual architectural specimens such as fatsia, palms and tree ferns. Closer to the ground succulents such as sedums, sempervivums and echeverias with their fleshy leaves create an interesting tapestry of contrasting textures. Some of the most popular types of evergreen are the spring flowering shrubs such as rhododendrons and camellias that love acid soil. Another very popular shrub is bay which is often grown as a standard, with its fragrant leaves being used to flavour dishes. Of course many evergreen shrubs are shaped into

Previous page Flower border with mixed perennials and annuals at Nymans, West Sussex

Below Evergreen foliage can be used to create an intriguing tapestry of contrasting textures.

topiary or can be used to create intricate knot gardens. Whatever evergreens you plant they can be used as key building blocks in planting schemes and form the backbone of many garden designs.

Some of the most popular evergreen plants (see also Conifers and Ferns) are listed here:

Choisya ternata 'Sundance' – although classified as 'evergreen' the leaves on this shrub are bright yellow, making a useful, permanent splash of colour in the garden. An added bonus is that the leaves have a spicy fragrance when crushed, rather reminiscent of pesto. It produces clusters of fragrant white flowers in summer.

Photinia x *fraseri* 'Red Robin' – a popular evergreen shrub due to its amazing flush of red foliage on the juvenile growth. It is easy to grow and makes an attractive feature when grown on its own, but is often used as a colourful hedge. It is also occasionally grown as a standard plant (single trunk with lollipop-like head of foliage).

Aucuba japonica – this is a tough old shrub with attractive, spotted, leathery leaves, hence its common name 'spotted laurel'. Easy to grow and happy in sun or shade, it is drought tolerant making it a useful plant for 'greening' up urban locations.

Euonymus fortunei 'Silver Queen' – this is a great plant with a lax habit making it perfect for sprawling around at the front of shrub borders or up walls and fences. There are a number of different euonymus shrubs with varying foliage colour, but 'Silver Queen' has dark green leaves with silvery white edges. In winter the foliage takes on an attractive pinkish glow. It forms small, creamy white flowers in summer.

Garrya elliptica 'James Roof' – a wonderful architectural shrub that reminds me of something you would use on a Gothic film set. Often used to drape a shady

Above Hedges are useful for dividing up spaces within a garden and providing a strong structural backbone element to many designs.

wall it is an attractive evergreen shrub with greyish green leathery leaves. It is in winter that it comes into its own with its amazing long, pendant green catkins.

Skimmia japonica 'Rubella' – skimmias are easy-to-grow shrubs, with both female plants that produce bright red berries, and male plants that produce fragrant flowers. 'Rubella' is male and slow growing making it ideal for the front of a shrub border or for growing in a pot for year-round interest.

Conifers

Conifers are one of the most popular groups of evergreen trees for hedging and screening, and there is a huge range that can be grown in the garden, from gigantic forest trees through to tiny, ground-hugging species. Whatever the size of outdoor space you have, there is always room for a conifer. Nearly all conifers are evergreen, but there are some exceptions such as the deciduous *Ginkgo biloba*, *Larix decidua* (European larch), *Taxodium distichum* (swamp cypress) and *Metasequoia glyptostroboides* (dawn redwood).

Conifers have previously suffered from an image problem, with many designers associating them with an out-of-date, 1970s style of gardening, but they are back with a vengeance. They have once again found popularity amongst gardeners for their wonderful textural qualities and for providing a permanent planting structure.

Some conifers such as leylandii have also suffered from a bad press due to their fast growing habit and large size, meaning neighbouring gardens and houses have had their light blocked out. However, with careful selection and planning, conifers can be used to enhance a garden and create privacy without upsetting the

Below Strong, upright structures such as these clipped conifers, act as bold focal points and add a touch of formality to any garden.

neighbours. Some of them have dramatic or artistic shapes and garden designers use them to great effect, such as the pencil-thin *Juniperus scopulorum*, which can be strategically placed along a path to punctuate it with upright accents. The permanent grey-blue foliage makes a colourful statement and its skinny contours make it ideal for a gardener wanting something evergreen with height but not wanting to compromise on space.

One of the most popular conifers is the English yew tree, *Taxus baccata*, which can be used as a focal point in a garden when grown on its own, or it can make an attractive, dense, formal hedge. A good alternative is the Irish yew, which has a fastigiated shape (thin and upright), which can be a better alternative for a smaller garden. The golden version (Irish golden yew) *Taxus baccata* 'Fastigiata Aurea' has attractive golden foliage. *Cupressus macrocarpa* 'Gold Crest', has a conical habit and striking golden foliage with a wonderful lemony scent when crushed. It reaches around 5m (16½ft) tall after about ten years.

As a rule of thumb, many conifers won't respond well if pruned back hard into older wood, although there are some exceptions, such as yew and sometimes thuja, which usually react by making strong bushy growth.

HEDGING PLANTS

Hedges can transform a garden by providing structure and defining space, yet there are many different styles to choose from ranging from very formal, clipped yew hedges with precise lines, to mixed wild hedges that can be seen in lots of cottage gardens. Hedges can be used to define boundaries, whether within your own areas of garden, or between yourself and a neighbour. They can also be used to create small, intimate spaces or to mark out pathways and draw the eye down towards a certain object or feature. Screening unsightly areas of the garden such as a shed or compost site is also another reason for planting a hedge. Finally, some hedges can be a wonderful habitat for wildlife, providing them with a place to forage or nest in.

Most hedges are planted in two parallel lines in a zig-zag pattern to make it as a dense as possible. The best time to plant a hedge is in autumn when the soil is warm enough to allow the roots to settle before their growth in spring. The area should be dug over prior to planting and plenty of organic matter added.

Hedges can vary in size from large, vigorous leylandii types as tall as a house to small, compact, box hedges, such as in a knot garden, which only reach about knee height.

Avoid cutting hedges from spring through to midsummer if possible to prevent disturbing nesting birds. Hedges are usually cut in late summer or early autumn. Any earlier and it will mean having to give them another cut later on in the year.

Avoid cutting large-leaved hedges such as laurel with a hedge cutter if possible as this leaves ragged-looking leaves. Instead use secateurs or hand shears to give a better finish.

Types of hedge

Beech – a deciduous hedge, although it can hold onto its leaves for the majority of winter, making it useful for screening. Light green leaves for most of the year, turning a lovely coppery yellow colour in autumn.

Hornbeam – similar looking to beech but forms a slightly more compact hedge and the leaves are more serrated. Great for semi-formal areas of the garden.

Yew – a popular evergreen hedge, which forms a dark green backdrop. Often used in formal gardens, it adds an elegant, classy feel to any garden and makes a dense screen.

Mixed hedge – often used in informal or cottage gardens, a mixed hedge is brilliant for biodiversity. They usually contain a selection from hawthorn, blackthorn, wild roses, elder and holly to give a good mix of evergreen and deciduous plants with lots of berries and flowers at various times in the year.

IMPACT PLANTS

There are certain plants that make an enormous statement or impact in the garden simply by being planted because they have the wow factor. Sometimes it is just because of their size, while at other times it can be because they have striking foliage or huge flowers. It could also be because they have been planted in a prominent position that draws the eye, making them the key feature in the garden. Either way, impact plants in a garden are by their nature attention-seekers, bold and eye-catching, making them great features or focal points. Impact plants can either be planted on their own or can be accompanied by complementary plants, which enhance the feature.

There are many plants that can be used as an impact plant, including black bamboos, banana plants, tree ferns, cordylines and acers, and some of the most popular are listed below:

Trachycarpus fortunei – the Chinese windmill palm, is an evergreen plant that adds a touch of the exotic to the garden, eventually forming into a small tree with a chunky fibrous trunk and large, fan-shaped palm leaves that can grow up to 1m (3ft) wide. It is one of the hardier palms and a great impact plant for creating a focal point in the centre of a border or as a stand-alone feature in the lawn. It is also suitable for growing in a container on a warm, sunny patio. An alternative hardy palm to try is *Chamaerops humilis*, which forms masses of fan-shaped palm

Opposite above This very formal design cleverly uses two contrasting colours to create an extra element of interest in the garden.

Opposite below Trachycarpus fortunei are fairly hardy palms but always add a touch of the exotic to a garden, as well as additional height.

leaves about 50cm (20in) wide and grows into a compact, bushy, evergreen shrub.

Catalpa bignonioides – a wonderful impact plant due to its huge leaves and quirky blue-podded fruit. Although it can eventually grow into a largish tree it can be kept compact by cutting it back each year to near ground level. This encourages lots of new shoots and the leaves are even bigger. It's a wonderful plant for the back of the border or as a stand-alone feature in the garden. A similar plant with large foliage is *Paulownia tomentosa* but this will also form a large tree if left unpruned.

Phormium tenax – commonly known as New Zealand flax, is a striking, clump-forming perennial grown for its impressive foliage, which is leathery, strap-like and dark greyish green although there are lots of varieties with various colours. It makes a great statement as it will eventually grow to about 4m (13ft) and can be planted either in the back of a border or grown in a container. A similar plant to try is *Astelia chathamica* 'Silver Spear' with leathery, strap-like foliage, but it only grows to half the height.

Topiary is another example of an impact plant that can be used to striking effect in the garden. There are numerous different types of plants that can be used to shape or sculpt structures, but the most popular are English yew (*Taxus bacata*) for larger features or box (*Buxus sempervivens*) for smaller topiary shapes. If using box, be aware of the fungus box blight that can kill the plants. A good alternative to box is *Ilex crenata* (Japanese holly), which has similar small, evergreen leaves and is just as suitable for sculpting into intricate shapes.

Topiary can be made into any shape and you can be as free as you like to use your imagination to sculpt something personal to you in the garden using a pair of edging shears. Some of the most common shapes are spheres, pyramids and swirling uprights, but use your creative and artistic skills to create something more exciting. It is great fun experimenting.

GRASSES AND BAMBOOS

A garden design based predominantly around grasses or bamboos or both is the ultimate in experimenting with form and texture, unencumbered by the distraction of colour. This is gardening at its most nuanced, with the added advantage of being relatively easy to care for. It is sometimes possible to do little more than take a hedge trimmer to it once a year.

Tranquil when the air is still, in high winds, grasses and bamboos rustle and bow to every breeze and gust like living anemometers, and even in relatively small spaces, carefully chosen plants can give a lush and exotic feel, hiding boundaries and creating mysterious depth, sound and movement. On a smaller scale adding grasses to your borders will have a similar effect. They are especially useful for

Opposite Grasses can be used to great effect in the borders, not only looking good but adding movement and sound as they rustle in the breeze.

Below The colourful stems of bamboo can be just as striking as the most brightly coloured flowers

adding light, airy height rather than solid bulk, as many other garden shrubs would do.

The most important consideration when choosing a bamboo is to research their invasive potential. Many bamboos will spread rapidly, taking over swathes of your garden, or coming up in paths or other unwanted places. It is possible to limit their spread by containing them in the ground in some way, but, if space is an issue, it is better to find varieties that are well behaved rather than risk an invasion.

Phyllostachys nigra, the black bamboo, is clump forming and relatively slow spreading so is fairly easy to control. Its canes turn jet black after a season's growth, best seen if the lower leaves are cut off to expose the colour, and it is wonderfully elegant. The slightly more unruly golden bamboo, *P. aurea*, also provides colourful stems that will reach to around 6–8m (20–26ft) tall. Equally, there are good dwarf varieties available, such as *Pleioblastus variegatus* or *P. viridistratus* to add metre-high variegated foliage to a shady spot.

Grasses also come in a wide variety of sizes and shapes suitable for both damp shade and dry, sunny conditions and it is impossible to list them all here. As a starting point try cultivars of miscanthus, with silky, fan-shaped plumes making lovely, elegant plants that reach around 1.5m (5ft) high. In sunny areas the stipa family are just superb. *Stipa gigantea's* tall 2m (6½ft) stems will drip with golden teardrops, which sparkle with the sun behind them, whilst *S. tenuissima*, the angel hair grass, only reaches around 50cm (20in) high but its soft silkiness was surely made to run one's hands through.

For interesting colour the Japanese blood grass, *Imperata cylindrical* 'Rubra' cannot be beaten, its small clumps turning bright red in summer before dying down, or try the black lily grass, *Ophiopogon planiscapus* 'Nigrescens', interspersed with low growing, silver foliage plants for best effect.

FERNS

The likelihood is that any ferns in your garden have popped up unexpectedly entirely of their own will. Yet ferns have a quiet and cool charm that brings calm elegance to the garden, especially where shade might be an issue, and deserve to be given more consideration.

The Victorians were obsessed with ferns to an extraordinary degree, creating damp corners and false landscapes designed especially to show off their textural forms and shapes. The classic Victorian fernery was a masterpiece of Gothic gloom, febrile and wild, a place where ghosts might wander and doomed lovers might meet, but today's sensibility is more concerned with elegance and structure than suppressed desire.

Ferns are considered to be the perfect plant for shade and they are certainly the masters of this particularly difficult micro-climate but they do not all need to be confined to the darkest places. Bracken, *Pteridium aquilinum*, is a fern, after all, but grows seemingly wherever it chooses, invading sunny pastures and deciduous woods alike. Having said that, ferns do make perfect specimens for a typical city dweller's back garden, where overhanging trees, walls and buildings often prevent any real sunshine getting through, or as underplanting in a woodland setting.

There are any number of fern varieties available, some of which are extremely happy in dry shade, always the most difficult micro-climate for the gardener, while others, such as *Osmunda regalis*, the royal fern, with its distinct shuttlecock shape, prefer damper conditions.

For dry shade, under trees or in the lee of walls, tough, hardy varieties, such as *Dryopteris felix-mas*, the deciduous male fern, or the paler, evergreen soft shield fern, *Polystichum setiferum*, will happily unfold their fronds. Or for something different, try *Adiantum venustum*, with its mass of triangular leaflets on wiry black stems on a damp bank, or the fashionable Japanese painted fern, *Athyrium niponicum* var. *pictum*, which comes in a variety of metallic purple, bronze and grey colours.

If you are lucky enough to live in a mild, maritime climate, you may also be able to grow the biggest of all the ferns, *Dicksonia antartica*, the tree fern, which is guaranteed to impress anyone.

Opposite above The fresh green colour of ferns can be used to dramatic effect, creating interesting textures and shapes.

Opposite below left Ferns are one of the earliest forms of plants and nothing looks quite as pre-historic and dramatic as its unfurling fronds.

Opposite below right A bold clump of shuttlcock ferns creates a cool and soothing effect in an herbaceous border.

Types of Gardens

Dry gardens

Drought tolerant plants are much more varied and interesting than one would imagine. As well as the obvious desert-style plants, like the succulents, it is also worth looking at the shrubs and perennials that cover the rocky slopes around the Mediterranean, known to some as the '*garrigue*'. Add to this many South African and American species and you should find enough plants to inspire and stimulate even in the driest of gardens.

Plants like this are an excellent choice if your garden is essentially dry and barren or a steep, rocky bank, but they are also useful around a patio, as this is often an area that gets reduced rainfall due to proximity to the house. Many also love life in a pot and will not mind being forgotten about or left untended whilst you jet off on your summer holiday.

Succulents such as the *Aeonium*, especially the black 'Swartkop' are always achingly stylish and their rosettes are eye-catching, whether individually planted in a pot or as a forest of windmill-topped tree shapes. Alongside these the bush aloes of South Africa always look good. Their extra bulk will cover the ground well while the flowers, resembling red hot pokers, another good choice, come in a variety of vibrant colours – yellow through orange to red. They are not fully hardy so may need winter protection or winter storage if frost is a problem. If you want to be really brave there are some cacti that cope with a little frost, mostly from the *Opuntia* family, the prickly pear cactus, which again may need protection in cold and wet conditions.

If cacti aren't your thing then the agave family makes a good substitute. Statuesque and dramatic plants, they are especially good on a slope, where their shape can be admired from a distance, thus avoiding any contact with the sharp spines! The most common and hardiest is *Agave americana*, with its blue-green colour. If space is an issue there are also some smaller puyas from Chile, which have a similar look and great flowers eventually, but they nearly all have incredibly vicious spines.

Luckily there are other plants to choose from for a softer landscape look. These are mostly from around the Mediterranean, where rocky hillsides tumble down towards the azure sea, hot, drying winds occasionally scour the landscape and the sun beats down every day.

As a group Mediterranean plants tend to be evergreen, low growing and shrubby with tough leaves, often silver or hairy, and a great many of them are aromatic

Opposite above left
Succulents such as the Aenonium, 'Swartkop' with their eye-catching foliage make great features in pots but will need protection in cooler areas of the country.

Opposite above right
There is nothing better than Osteospermums for brightening up a dull corner.

Opposite below A sea of blue lavender can cope growing in poor soil.

as well as free flowering. Plants such as lavender, thyme and sage thrive in dry conditions, especially in gravelled areas alongside the more potent wormwood and rue. Varieties of phlomis and cistus, dry-loving shrubs from even further south, will add some height and bulk as well as an endless succession of flowers, and look wonderful when planted with olive trees. For really bright colour, the South African daisies, such as lampranthus and osteospermum, can quickly spread over even the poorest, rockiest of soil, especially in milder areas.

Woodland gardens

Not everybody has room for a full-blown woodland garden, but a lovely shady area where a few choice woodland plants thrive, can be made in the smallest of areas. All that you need is a small tree canopy, a middle storey of shrubs and some ground cover. Finally, adding bulbs will complete the woodland theme. This will provide lots of interest throughout the year and will also attract wildlife.

Above Acers are one of the best trees to ensure you have an autumnal punch of foliage colour in your woodland garden.

Starting with a tree canopy, choose a tree that won't get too big but will provide some upright interest and cast dappled shade onto the ground below, replicating the woodland floor. Birch trees are a good choice in a small garden as their stark white trunks instantly provide interest all year round. Because of their narrow shape, there is often room for three trees planted closely together, ideal for a small garden. Other trees worth considering are *Acer palmatum* to provide attractive autumn colour, or some of the snakebark acer types to provide trunk interest. Malus or cherry trees will provide two seasons of interest; blossom in spring and berries in winter. Another good choice is a sorbus, such as the rowan tree, which also has springtime flowers and attractive fruit later in the year.

For additional interest you can train climbers, such as wisteria, clematis, hop or honeysuckle up into the tree.

In the middle canopy, typical woodland plants will include rhododendrons and camellias (if you have slightly acidic soil), which thrive in the dappled shade of deciduous trees. Other shrubs you could consider include skimmia, buddleja, hawthorn or blackthorn.

In the lower canopy plant low growing plants such as *Vinca* 'Dartington Star' or even wild strawberries. Epimediums are another good choice for light shade, or you could try some ferns. Finally, add some bulbs such as snowdrops, bluebells or crocus, and your woodland garden is complete.

Coastal gardens

Gardeners who love to be beside the seaside may enjoy wonderful views and the odd refreshing paddle in the sea but they have to face a very specific set of conditions and weather-related issues that can have a major impact on plant choice and cultivation.

On the one hand maritime climates do tend to be milder and more humid, with less risk of frost, especially if they are south- or west-facing and enjoying the benefits of the warm ocean currents of the Atlantic jet stream. However, the price paid for this is an increase in exposure to wind, often laden with leaf-scorching salt and strong enough to flatten any soft, sappy plants you may have.

If you can bear to lose a little of that splendid view, planting windbreaks to reduce the effect of the wind will help enormously. Depending on the size of your garden there are both trees and shrubs known to tolerate salt and wind. Sycamores, oaks and pines or the smaller hawthorn all do the job well, as do tamarisk, *Tamarix tetrandra*, a deciduous shrub with fluffy pink flowers in summer, and the sea buckthorn, *Hippophae rhamnoides*, with its orange berries. A good windbreak should reduce the wind speed and the salt tremendously without causing extra turbulence as a more solid structure would. If these don't appeal or you have a smaller garden, the wilder shrub roses, such as *Rosa rubiginosa* make an excellent substitute.

Behind this shelterbelt there are many other plants tolerant of these conditions as long as they are not completely exposed to winds. Shrubs like the hardy *Fuchsia magellanica*, *escallonia* and *olearia* from New Zealand and easy-to-grow perennials, such as crocosmia and achillea will all do well as will many of the lower growing ornamental grasses.

In the mildest, west-facing gardens of the West Country, Scotland and Ireland the moisture-laden air is perfect for plants from China, the Himalayas and the mountains of Chile. Tree ferns, trachycarpus palms and camellias will all thrive in sheltered positions, protected from frost and scorching wind.

Below The herbaceous perennial achillea is a good choice for a coastal garden although it will benefit with shelter from prevailing wind.

Sub-tropical gardens

Some areas of Britain are lucky enough to enjoy an almost sub-tropical climate for much of the year. Others less so but with a little extra work can achieve a sub-tropical effect during the summer months at least by clever planting combinations. Sub-tropical gardens are characterised by large-leaved plants and bright-coloured, exotic-looking flowers, as well as by a variety of special plants so if you do garden in a frost-prone area, choose hardy shrubs and plants, that have these features as the basis for your design, and you can then drop in some of the more challenging plants in between when the weather conditions suit.

Good backbone plants for a sub-tropical scheme are trees and shrubs, such as *Fatsia japonica* and *Cordyline australis*, the Torbay palm. Both are pretty hardy and will take some frost. Phormiums in a range of colours also add to the dramatic effect and most will survive a cold winter with ease. For a really big-leaved tropical effect a few banana species are reliably hardy, most notably *Musa basjoo*, although it will need to be cut down following frost and protected from the winter rain in less amenable areas. Underplanting with hostas and ferns will also add to the lush feel.

For flowers, cannas, such as the bronze-leaved *Canna* 'Wyoming', dahlias, agapanthus and fuchsia can be potted up and dropped into any spaces in the

Left If you live in a really sheltered area, you could even get bananas flowering producing small (inedible) fruits.

Above Creating an exotic or subtropical-style garden often requires lots of plants with lush foliage as well as brightly coloured flowers.

summer months to add some extra colour, while bedding plants like the New Guinea impatiens can also be planted at the front for an immediate splash of brightness.

If you are fortunate enough to garden in a mild area in the south or west then you can add many more properly sub-tropical species to your design. Palm trees, such as *Trachycarpus fortunei*, the Chusan palm with its furry trunk, or the fan palm, *Chaemerops humilis*, are both easy to grow in these conditions but it is also worth trying to find one of the blue-leaved palms, like the Mexican blue palm, *Brahea armata*, to give that extra edge. You will also have a greater choice of bananas to play with, including *Ensete ventricosum* 'Maurelii' with its extraordinary red, striped markings.

One last classic sub-tropical plant with the biggest leaves of them all deserves a special mention, but it does require a damp situation, preferably next to a stream. *Gunnera manicata*, the giant ornamental rhubarb, is simply stunning, with leaves that can shelter whole families from the rain but it needs a large space to show itself off so this is not a plant for a small back garden. There are, admittedly, smaller cultivars available but they never have the same dramatic effect as this monster.

PRODUCTIVE GARDENS

There is nothing more rewarding in the horticultural world than growing your own fruit and veg at home. Not only does it taste so much better than anything you can buy in the supermarket, but it is practically free (except for the price of a packet of seeds) and there is a much wider range of crops to choose from than you can find in the shops.

Kitchen gardens can look beautiful too. They can be crammed full of flowers, ornamental fruit trees and lots of contrasting shapes, textures and colours from the different types of vegetables that can be grown. The French use the word '*potager*' derived from *potage* (soup) to describe an ornamental kitchen garden where flowers and edible crops jostle for position as a stunning concoction in a beautiful garden display.

With regard to fruit, it is easy to grow trees in small spaces. Most fruit trees can be grown in containers, or if they are grown on dwarfing rootstocks, can be grown against a fence or wall, taking up hardly any space at all. Popular shapes for growing fruit trees on a fence include fans, cordons and espaliers, all of which look beautiful in the garden. Low growing 'step-over' apple trees, literally up to knee height, are also a wonderful way of cramming small fruit trees into a tiny space. Closer to the ground there are a wonderful array of fruit bushes such as gooseberries, blackberries and redcurrants, all of which look beautiful when laden with brightly coloured fruit. Strawberries and tomatoes are also easy to grow and can even be grown in hanging baskets.

With regard to vegetables, nearly everything can be grown in containers if space is at a premium. Cut and come again lettuce or rows of carrots and radishes can even be grown in window boxes. Climbers such as runner and French beans make beautiful floral displays when scrambling up wigwam structure, which will rival any clematis in terms of beauty. Other plants such as Jerusalem artichokes produce flowers as good as any sunflower, and globe artichokes as ornamental as a cardoon.

Remember to leave room somewhere for a compost heap as this is the essential powerhouse of the productive garden, enabling you to recycle garden waste and transform it into lovely compost to put back onto your beds and nourish your plants.

Opposite Apple trees not only provide you with delicious fruits, but can be trained into all sorts of elaborate shapes such as this espalier.

Above left Vegetable gardens can look beautiful as well as be productive, providing colour with foliage and flowers.

Above right Growing your own food is extremely rewarding, giving you tasty and healthy food for the cost of a packet of seeds.

CUTTING GARDENS

Many people do like to bring a bit of their garden inside with them, whether to save money or just for pride's sake. Having an area for cut flowers may seem to be an extravagance but it will give you the opportunity to produce bigger and better arrangements all year round, without spoiling the effect of your main displays.

There is probably little point in growing your greenery separately, as your garden, in all likelihood, already has a range of shrubs that make a perfect backdrop to your blooms. Cutting a few bits and pieces off most shrubs is unlikely to be noticeable and it means that you can fill your vase with plenty of plant life for free and save your pennies for the star flowers that will form the centrepiece.

If you have philadelphus (mock orange), viburnums, forsythia, lilac and hydrangea, or holly, ivy, cotoneaster or pyracantha for autumn and winter, you have plenty of ingredients available. Climbers such as honeysuckle, clematis and jasmine are also useful, as are interesting twiggy shrubs. Contorted willow or hazel smothered in catkins look amazing and give any flower display height and form.

A cutting garden area is probably better used for growing plants that are easy and relatively cheap to grow but would cost considerably more to buy, or for flowers that you may love, but which don't really fit elsewhere in your garden. Huge dinner plate dahlias or multi-toned gladioli look fabulous in an arrangement but may not fit well with the other plants in garden borders.

For lots and lots of blooms sowing seeds is your best bet. Rows of plants like cosmos, snapdragon, larkspur, nigella (better known as love-in-a-mist) and sweet peas take very little effort, apart from the endless sweet pea picking, which is at least a rather lovely, fragrant activity. Sunflowers are also wonderful, and then there are interesting annuals like honesty, physalis and annual grasses *Hordeum jubatum*, the squirrel grass.

The advantage of growing in rows is twofold. It makes it much easier to pick an armful of flowers at speed and you can support lax plants very easily and quickly without individual staking. Before the plants actually flower place a row of stakes along the middle and gently weave string in a figure of eight back and forward to catch the greenery and hold everything upright.

Perennials and bulbs may cost a little more and take up space but are worth investing in for a more sophisticated feel. Dahlias are just the best plant ever for cutting as your plants will just produce more blooms. Delphinium, campanulas and almost every daisy-type perennial will all last well in a vase, as do alstroemeria and, at least in the cutting garden, their laxity is less of a problem than in the border. The perennial gypsophilia is also a very useful plant, if you can find it, with plenty of branching stems to add billowing clouds of pretty baby's breath flowers to set off the bigger, more substantial flowers.

Opposite above left
The pretty perennial gypsophilia, commonly known as baby's breath, has lots of branching stems of delicate, cloud-like flowers.

Opposite above right
Sunflowers are one of the classic annuals, often seen in a cut flower border.

Opposite below Sweet peas are a popular cut flower plant that love scrambling up rustic-looking wigwam structures, while the blue spikes of delphiniums are another favourite among florists.

ELEMENTS OF DESIGN

DESIGNING WITHIN A SPACE

Creating a beautiful garden is not just about picking out some 'perfect plants' and throwing them together in any order. A well-designed garden is the sum of all its parts; how those plants fit into the landscape and work alongside each other is just one of the factors that enhances the experience. There are various elements that should be thought about in the overall design in the same way an artist composes a painting. Some of the key elements to consider include shape, texture and form, colour, symmetry and of course the overall style of the garden you are wishing to create. Think of the individual plants as the building blocks for your design, but remember that there are a whole lot of other considerations in the overall picture.

Design is ultimately subjective, but there are a few basics that will help you get the right feel for the garden. After that, you can use your imagination and artistic flair to create something wonderful.

Probably the most important element in the design of the garden is its overall shape. While the outer boundary may be fixed, how you position and design the areas, beds and borders within is much more flexible and open to experiment. One aspect to avoid, yet it is surprisingly common, is a large, open, empty space in the centre, such as a lawn or patio, with tiny, narrow flower beds around the outside, pushed up against the fence. It can look as if a huge centrifugal force has spun and forced all your lovely plants to the outer corners. Instead of showing off your plants you will have created a dull, featureless vista, unbalanced and mean-looking, so unless you really do need to make room for the equivalent of a football pitch in the centre, try making your beds bold and large, filled with overflowing flowers and foliage. Let the plants take centre stage.

Line is an essential element of garden design. Consider how flower beds can direct our view. Symmetry and straight parallel lines, such as two borders, are great for doing this, leading the eye onwards and away towards a point in the distance or another feature. However, using curves rather than straight lines to give more sweeping vistas can completely change the feel, slowing the experience down as the curves are followed. Large, voluptuous and asymmetric curves can be exciting, giving a sense of generosity and abundance, so don't be afraid to experiment. Like water, people tend to move faster in long, narrow areas, and then slow down in wider openings, a phenomenon known as 'challenging and pooling'. Make the most of this to manipulate and encourage interest.

A key tip is to remember is that vertical lines running down the length will make a garden feel much longer than it really is, whereas horizontal lines across will make it seem wider. This is useful if the proportions of your space are a little off.

Important, too, is creating a sense of intrigue. For example, you can have a path that disappears off around the corner and out of view. Even if that path leads to a dead end, the overall feel is that there is more to explore and that the garden is bigger than it really is. Ancient Japanese designers mastered this art in their gardens and called it *miegakure* or 'hide and reveal'. Views are hinted at or partially revealed but not everything is immediately on show.

Other tricks to make a garden feel bigger can include placing outdoor mirrors in strategic places to reflect back the existing garden. Mirrors can also be used to show off a different angle of a feature plant, or giving the illusion of double the amount of plants and enhancing the effect of colour and texture. Planting small trees or shrubs along a border can also make something seem much longer than it really is if they are in descending sizes as this exaggerates our sense of proportion and perspective.

Above Woodland gardens look best when designed to look as natural as possible, such as these bluebells under the canopy of a tree.

Opposite Try to ensure that a garden design includes as many elements as possible, such as colour, texture, height and a well-proportioned space.

DESIGNING WITH PLANTS

Once you have the basic shape and layout of your garden mapped out then you can concentrate on your planting combinations. As a rule of thumb, taller plants should go towards the back and smaller ones at the front. However, do bear in mind that plants appear at different times of the year so sometimes lower plants can be placed further back if later they'll be hidden by taller ones.

A design without strong, contrasting form can become confusing and insipid, lacking rhythm or focus. Careful planning, that takes account of the form and shape of plants and other objects in the garden, will give your design a necessary backbone, the skeleton that the rest of your plants can hang from. Use strong, defined forms to divide or enclose space, to create points of interest or to draw the eye, to break up the view or to link it together.

Grouping structural plants in certain ways can help to create specific effects. So a series of mounded forms brings gentle rhythm and definition, for example, while a cluster of repeated, narrow verticals will provide a sense of solidity and completeness, where one upright vertical statement plant may look out of place and exposed.

Texture, too, can provide visual repetition and unity as well as contrast, but it is also an invitation to other senses, to touch and interact with the garden. This deep-rooted, primitive, emotional response creates all sorts of connections and memories, as does scent, increasing a garden's appeal tremendously.

Of course, many designers and gardeners are fixated on colour, and this is obviously a key ingredient in garden design. If you get your colour combinations right, they will transform a mediocre space into something magical. Colour can be used to create a mood, an ambiance, or simply seduce the soul with its visual impact. However, get it wrong and everything seems to jar and clash and the experience may be ruined.

Hot, fiery colours, such as reds, yellows and oranges bring vibrancy and warmth to a planting scheme, whereas softer pastel colours of blues, whites and mauves seem cooler and more relaxing. Sometimes borders will start off with hot colours and move down to the cooler ones. This gives the effect of making the border feel longer than it really is, as hot colours always feel closer than they are, while cool ones have the appearance of being further away.

Too many colours can look haphazard and chaotic. Too few can look dull and muted. So getting the right amount or balance of colours and tones is important, although some gardens, such as the famous White Garden at Sissinghurst, are successfully planted using just a single colour to create a specific look.

Designers use colours in different ways. Some like to use blocks, drifts or swathes

Opposite Even fruit and veg gardens can look good if careful consideration is given to the design of the overall space.

Below Try not to use too many colours in a design as this can look over-complicated and messy. This simple combination of just blue and yellow works well.

of individual colours alongside each other. Others like to create rhythm in a border by repeating the same colour pattern.

Some colours work better together than others, and if you are unsure about a particular combination you can always refer to a colour wheel. Originally created by Isaac Newton in 1666, this is a circle based on the three primary colours of red, yellow and blue, and then broken down further into secondary and tertiary colours. Generally colours next to each other on the wheel will provide a smooth transition if used in the design of a border – red to orange, for example, whereas opposite colours often create the biggest complementary contrast, and can have the biggest impact, like yellow with violet.

Finally to style. In all likelihood this will be a reflection of your personality and needs. Overall it helps to choose a style that reflects the existing hardscaping around you. For example, a cottage garden, with rambling roses, loose planting schemes and mixed colour is an ideal choice for a garden in the countryside, while a town house may suit a formal-style garden with straight, hard lines incorporating structured symmetry. There are no hard and fast rules though, and sometimes clever contrasts between soft and hard landscaping style can be both provoking and inspired.

INDEX

Acknowledgments

I would particularly like to thank Ali Marshall (head gardener of Torre Abbey, Torquay) for help with researching the text and providing the wonderful artwork.

Also, a massive thank you to all the National Trust gardeners from around the country that gave me plenty of tips and advice along the way as well as lots of encouragement. Also to those that supplied photos.

Thank you to Peter Taylor from Pavilion Books for having the passion and vision to come up with the idea for this National Trust book and to senior editor Jocelyn Norbury for her superb editing and project management skills and being able to translate my scribblings into something readable.

Thank you to my family Annabel, Guy, Lissie and Hugh for putting up with me for another year while I typed away in the garden room. And to my springers Beanie and River for keeping me company, patiently sitting by my feet under the desk while I burnt the midnight oil.

Finally I would like to dedicate this book to all those wild and intrepid plant hunters in the past that risked their lives so that we could enjoy the simple pleasure of watching these wonderful plants grow in our gardens.